Self-Harm

A psychotherapeutic approach

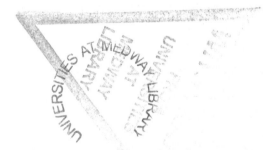

Fiona Gardner

Brunner-Routledge
Taylor & Francis Group

HOVE AND NEW YORK

First published 2001 by Brunner-Routledge
27 Church Road, Hove, East Sussex, BN3 2FA

Simultaneously published in the USA and Canada
by Taylor & Francis Inc
29 West 35th Street, New York, NY 10001

Reprinted 2002

Reprinted 2004
by Brunner-Routledge
27 Church Road, Hove, East Sussex, BN3 2FA
270 Madison Avenue, New York, NY 10016

Brunner-Routledge is an imprint of the Taylor & Francis Group

© 2001 Fiona Gardner

Typeset in Times by Keystroke, Jacaranda Lodge, Wolverhampton
Printed and bound in Great Britain by The Cromwell Press
This publication has been produced with paper manufactured to strict
environmental standards and with pulp derived from sustainable forests.

Cover design by Lisa Dynan

British Library Cataloguing in Publication Data
A catalogue record for this book is available from the British Library

Library of Congress Cataloging in Publication Data
A catalog record for this book is available from the Library of Congress

ISBN 0–415–22302–X (hbk)
ISBN 0–415–23303–8 (pbk)

Self-Harm

Cutting the skin, repeatedly and habitually, is worryingly common in many young women. Such self-harm is often used as a way of easing emotional suffering. How can we understand the reasons for this, and how do we help someone who thinks they already have a satisfactory way of dealing with distress?

Self-Harm: A Psychotherapeutic Approach explores the issues involved from the perspective of the psychoanalytical psychotherapist – with the conviction that there is more to the behaviour than the acts themselves. Drawing on her clinical experience with young women, Fiona Gardner shows how self-harm is characteristic of an adolescent state of mind with its conflicts involved in separation and sexuality. At a deeper level she examines the influence of unresolved desires originating from early object relations – how we mentally order early experience. She introduces as a central concept the idea of the 'encaptive conflict' in which self-harming young women are caught. These issues are looked at through extensive clinical material, and are combined with an analysis of the social and cultural influences behind self-harm.

This book is aimed at all those working, or training to work, with those who are harming themselves, including psychotherapists, school counsellors, GP counsellors, social workers and mental health clinicians, as well as counsellors and therapists working in voluntary agencies and community projects.

Fiona Gardner is a psychoanalytic psychotherapist and a training therapist and supervisor. She has been published in leading national and international psychotherapy journals on gender, sexual abuse and psychotherapy training, and has contributed to several books.

For Barbara Butler

Contents

Acknowledgements

I would like to thank all those patients whom I saw for psychotherapy at the clinic, especially those who raised both my concern and interest in self-harm, which eventually led to writing the book. I must also acknowledge my colleagues Dr Karen Boucher, Greg Dring and Jane Thomason, and the secretaries Anne Paterson and Lindy Elliot. I learned a great deal from clinical discussions both in individual and group supervision, and would like to thank Robin Balbernie, Dr Barbara Cottman, David Hadley and Sara Rance. Thank you also to Glenys James for her supervision skills and for her comments on Chapter 1.

Thanks to Lynne Bevan from the Birmingham University Field Archaeological Unit for sending such useful references and data. I am grateful to Herbert Hahn for his comments on early drafts of Chapter 6, and to Chris Williams for explaining and discussing Jungian ideas and terminology. Thanks also to Lois Arnold from the Basement Project, Abergavenny, for our conversation and the pioneering work of the Self-Injury Forum. I would like to thank Ann Scott for her expertise and advice and for her personal support.

A particular thank you to Peter Ellis for his work on the index, and for his intellectual and emotional support. Thanks also to Daniel Ellis and Gemma Ellis for their encouragement, and to friends who remained interested in my work.

I am grateful to Kate Hawes and the staff at Brunner-Routledge for their positive attitude and helpful advice.

Thanks go to Margaret Graham and Sue Anderson for permission to write about their experiences.

Some of the material in Chapter 3 was originally published as 'Echoes and repetitions' in *Changes* (1997) and I am grateful to John Wiley and Sons Limited for permission to include it.

Lyrics from 'Feeling Called Love' (Banks/Cocker/Doyle/Mackey/Senior/Webber). Copyright 1995 by kind permission of Universal/Island Music Ltd. I am grateful to the Modern Poetry Association for permission to reprint 'Pauline Is Falling' by Jean Nordhaus, which first appeared in *Poetry*, copyrighted March 2000, and is registered at the Library of Congress, Washington, DC.

PAULINE IS FALLING
   from the cliff's edge,
kicking her feet in panic and despair
as the circle of light contracts and blackness
takes the screen. And that
is how we leave her, hanging – though we know
she will be rescued, only to descend
into fresh harm, the story flowing on,
disaster and reprieve – systole, diastole – split
rhythm of a heart that hungers

only to go on.

                              (Jean Nordhaus)

Chapter 1

Introduction

> One comes to see that it is not so much the nature of the act that counts but its meaning.
>
> (Chasseguet-Smirgel 1990: 77)

This book is about uncovering the different meanings behind self-harm – a term used to describe self-inflicted physical attacks on the body. The central focus in this book is on cutting the surface of the skin, but there is also some reference to attacks such as burning and hitting the body. Implicit in the definition is an understanding that the body is going to be deliberately, and usually habitually, harmed rather than destroyed or killed, and that it is also a harming of the self. So why would people turn on their bodies in this way, repeatedly inflicting such painful damage on themselves?

> Feeling unreal and distant disconnected with life,
> I pick up my razor blades,
> Relieved at the sight of them I cry,
> Not totally aware I cut into the skin,
> Jolted back into reality by the act,
> Checking that I'm still alive that I'm still real,
> For a short while I am in control, for a short while I am at peace.

This poem was written by one of the young women with whom I worked. She knew why, as she writes, she had to cut herself – it helped her to know that she was alive, real and in control. I was concerned and affected by such actions, and needed to understand their impact and unconscious meanings. It was from this concern, and the relative lack of analytic literature on the subject, that the idea of this book arose. From the young woman who wrote the poem and others like her, it seemed that attacks on the body were felt to be attempts at coping and even at self-healing. Such an attack on the self was also clearly a gesture, albeit a paradoxical one, in that feelings of relief and of being alive came from inflicting pain on the body. From my psychotherapeutic practice I understood that the attacks were a metaphoric representation for earlier psychic wounds and internalised processes derived from early object relationships. Object relations is a key concept in psychoanalytic psychotherapy. It means that both our real experiences of and our fantasies about parental and other figures (objects) are internalised, and become embedded in the way we cope with life. These inner objects then pattern our psyches and influence other relationships and the way we behave. In that sense self-harm can be seen as a system of signs marking statements about the self, and past relationships and previous experiences.

However, it is not just a private matter. Generally in the social field and in the collective consciousness there is a powerful symbolism attached to drawing blood and marking the body, which can link to healing, salvation, social identity and order. Attacking the body is then a gesture, a representation and an action, involving paradox, metaphor and symbol.

Through psychoanalytic thinking and the practice of psychoanalytic psychotherapy, we can gain access to the unconscious mind and to the underlying function and motivations for our actions. With this perspective the conscious meaning has its counterpart of unconscious meaning – in other words, the deeper meaning which is underneath that which is knowingly meant. An analytic approach reveals the power and extent of the unconscious and our inner individual conflicts and needs, but analytic thinking also helps with an understanding of the family, the way groups function, the wider social field and our cultural heritage. In this book cutting is explored primarily from the perspective of the individual, but is also considered as a behaviour particularly found in adolescents, and with significance as part of a wider social and cultural context. All these aspects are fully explored and discussed.

Generally people feel that psychoanalytic psychotherapy is only for those who can afford it, or who are already articulate or psychologically minded. What I aim to show in this exploration of self-harm is that psychoanalytic thinking can influence the way we reflect about our work and the way we listen to patients, whatever the context, and whatever their or our background. In that way, this book is aimed at the broad sweep of those who are working and involved with people who harm themselves.

A word about the terms being used: 'self-harming behaviour', which is also sometimes referred to as self-injury, is different from self-mutilation, in that the term 'self-mutilation' tends to be used both in psychiatric and psychoanalytic writings to refer to serious and sometimes lethal body mutilations where the aim is often to actually cut off an offending body part. This is relatively rare in comparison to self-harming. An estimate about the known frequency of self-harm is generally quoted as one in 600 adults who harm themselves sufficiently to require hospital treatment, although this figure is acknowledged as probably an underestimate (Tantam and Whittaker 1992). A recent United States study (Strong 2000) gives a prevalence of one in eight students who had deliberately cut or burnt themselves. People who harm themselves will be found on the caseload of virtually every community-based professional. Interestingly there is a greater incidence in British social services and probation departments than the high-profile work with child neglect and abuse (Pritchard 1995). The extent of the behaviour creates great demand, leads to considerable unhappiness for all those involved, and results in high levels of attendance at accident and emergency departments. It is especially prevalent among adolescent girls and women, and there is a clear gender dimension that has to be considered in uncovering meaning. This is one of the central themes in the book.

This book draws on my experience of working first as a social worker in social services and child and family guidance for fourteen years, and second as a psychoanalytic psychotherapist for over twelve years, working initially for a voluntary organisation, and then in a public sector clinic for young people, as well as in private practice. The clinical work described in this book is taken mainly from my work in the clinic, but also from my private practice. The clinic was established on a tertiary referral basis – in other words, the young people who were seen had already been assessed either by a child and family psychiatry department or an adult mental health team, and then referred on to the clinic team. The rationale for establishing the specialist service was that it was hoped that more intensive work in the community would prevent admission to an adolescent residential unit or adult psychiatric ward. The young people referred were all showing serious signs of emotional disturbance and were often at risk. Many more females were referred – after eighteen months in operation the ratio was one-third young men to two-thirds young women, and the symptoms varied between the sexes. By far the largest group attending was of young women attacking their bodies – usually by a combination of methods which invariably included cutting.

Over a four-year period at the clinic, fifty-one young people were assessed with a view to psychotherapy, and of these I took on thirty-three for individual work. The remainder were offered another form of treatment within the clinic such as family work, cognitive therapy, or some joint therapeutic work between psychiatrist and psychiatric nurse involving close monitoring of the young person's weight or level of mental disturbance, others were referred on to another service, or dropped out. Out of the thirty-three seen for psychoanalytic psychotherapy, six were young men, only one of whom described suicidal thoughts; the others were referred with a variety of phobic and depressive symptoms. None of the young men were cutting themselves. Out of the twenty-seven young women taken on for individual psychotherapy, fifteen presented with symptoms that included cutting, although two of these hit themselves and another inflicted small burns on her body. Many cut alongside repeated overdosing, and some also had an eating disorder. Out of the remainder of the twenty-seven, six were referred for depression, three for drug use and three solely with an eating disorder. Such rough statistics do not of course constitute a valid scientific survey, so the grouping can in no way be seen as representative, but the preponderance of those who deliberately harmed themselves seemed to be significant and was a concern to myself and my colleagues.

The symptoms were repeated, and frequently included several other self-destructive behaviours alongside the cutting. Often the self-harm followed on from an earlier problem behaviour. There was clearly an addictive quality to the damaging actions, and, as mentioned, for some of the young women there was a well-established link both with overdosing and eating disorders. Out of those whose symptomatology included harming themselves, only one was cutting as the sole way of expressing her distress. Six were cutting and/or hitting themselves and had taken an overdose. One was cutting alongside her depression, and another burning herself and depressed, and four had an eating disorder alongside cutting. The two remaining had previously cut and then taken several overdoses, one also drank heavily and another misused drugs. Some of the young women also told of repeatedly putting themselves in dangerous situations, sometimes sexually and sometimes physically. While risk-taking behaviour is characteristic of the adolescent state of mind it is usually done in groups, and these young women tended to try things alone with minimum protection. Cutting was often one symptom among a chain of disorders, sometimes with one stopping and then being replaced by another.

The focus of this study is an exploration of the conscious and unconscious meanings that lay behind the self-cutting by the young women with whom I worked. Most people who harm themselves begin to do so in adolescence – a time of transition – and the focus of the clinical material used in this book is primarily, though not exclusively, based on psychotherapy with those aged between 15 and 21 years. Some of the clinical accounts involve older women who had begun harming themselves in adolescence. Cutting is in some ways seen as a particular characteristic of young adolescent females, and this aspect is explored here. All those who I saw were white, apart from one who was from the Far East.

A word about the actual injuries. When they cut themselves the young women created a wound using a sharp instrument, usually razors, sometimes knives. The areas they commonly cut were their arms and legs (usually their thighs), but some sometimes cut their stomach or breasts. The cutting made superficial, delicate and sometimes carefully designed incisions. Once the wound had healed, often no visible scar remained, but most of the young women tended to repeat the behaviour over and over again. Some cut more deeply, so unsightly scars were left or lumpy flesh formed around and over the wound. This sort of cutting is clearly different from making a single very deep wound around a jugular vein or radial artery. Burning was with cigarettes or cigarette lighters, and those who hit themselves either banged their heads or their hands, usually against walls – one so fiercely that her knuckles were bruised and damaged.

The frequency seemed periodic and sometimes even random, as the young women attacked themselves when they felt they needed to, and when they were upset and could not manage their feelings. Thus there were sometimes gaps of weeks, and sometimes months between incidents, while others reported cutting several times on a certain day, but were then able to have a space of several weeks before feeling that they needed to hurt themselves again. Generally the young women spoke of a sense of tension present immediately before they harmed themselves, and then different feelings either of numbness and/or gratification alongside the physical pain. There was normally a sense of shame and secrecy so that the scars were hidden under clothing. Mostly there were feelings of defeat, not self-possession or triumph, about what they had done.

As this book is an exploration of the conscious and unconscious meanings of attacking the body, it is not an outcome study. However, out of the fifteen young women with symptoms that included cutting, hitting and burning themselves, eight had stopped those symptoms by the time the psychotherapy ended, while with one it was not really clear. Three were unfortunately left with their long-established eating disorder, although the other forms of self-harm had stopped. Three left the area, so the treatment ended prematurely, and I later learned that one of these then took a serious, though not fatal, overdose.

Professionals in mental health – social workers, counsellors, teachers, families and friends, and by extrapolation the general public – seem to have a similar response to people who harm themselves, as was prevalent towards anorexics more than twenty years ago. This is generally one of shock, fear, anger, disgust and revulsion, which may lead to hostility and anxiety. Families and friends of those who are harming themselves are often deeply upset, and shocked by the behaviour. Sometimes this leads to denial – the idea that it is just a phase, something that will be grown out of – or sometimes parents may be too upset or angry to see beyond their own hurt feelings. Among professionals, such patients are seen as difficult, frustrating, and demanding of enormous amounts of professional attention. Why is the reaction so negative? There are obvious reasons, such as: the behaviour does not seem to make sense; it goes against current notions of health and attractiveness especially among young women; patients do not respond to drug treatment, or quick-fix psychological treatments; they demand time-consuming physical care for mental illness in contrast to those who are straightforwardly physically ill; they often do not know why they did it, or why they repeatedly do it, or seem to care about it, and so on.

What does this behaviour of attacking the body stir up within us? It may be that feelings of judgement and punishment which are evoked by such behaviour can serve as a defence against other upsetting feelings of horror, sadness, fear and responsibility for the person's well-being. Such feelings can be especially powerful if the professional lacks support or supervision of the work. Turp reminds us that the 'shocking' quality is an essential aspect of the behaviour, which communicates the rawness and unprocessed quality of the emotions and impulses (1999: 309).

Such feelings do not necessarily go away with familiarity, but over time they can become blunted and so easier to handle. Immediate feelings of shock are often followed by incomprehension and a search for direct meaning – if the injury can be explained, and a clear, obvious reason found for it, it becomes easier to cope with and understand. There can also be worries and fear about what the person might do next, and upset and distress at the pain the patient is causing to themselves. A common response is anger and frustration, particularly when the person continues to harm themselves during treatment, and such frustration leads to feelings of powerlessness and inadequacy in the therapist. If success is measured by symptoms, this can be problematic in situations where people continue to harm themselves, even though other changes have been made, and there is improvement.

One counsellor wrote:

When I first began to work with people who harmed themselves,
I was shocked and frightened. I also felt I should be able to stop them,
at least once we had established a therapeutic rapport. Surely they
should not need to do this to themselves when support and
opportunities to talk about things were on offer?

(*Self-Injury Forum Newsletter* 1999: 2)

So is self-harm a form of mental illness? The psychiatric literature
certainly includes it in a variety of diagnoses and classifications. Self-
harm is often linked to a manifestation of borderline personality disorder,
or to other 'multi-impulsive behaviours'. It is judged to be part of a
pathology found in patients who have difficulty in controlling their
impulses and coping with depressive feelings and anxiety. Histrionic,
narcissistic, schizotypal or antisocial personality disorder are all labels
that have been used, as has the more recent multi-impulsive personality
disorder. Self-harming behaviour is also said to be a possible symptom
of schizophrenia, major depression, mania, obsessive-compulsive disorder
and hypochondriasis. It is also recognised that cutting can occur in the
context of neurosis, and in response to situational crises, such as being
imprisoned or isolated.

All these various possibilities lead to a lack of coherence, and an
illusion that the behaviour is explained or even understood by the label.
A further problem is that by using such diagnoses the patient can become
reduced to her symptom. There is a tendency in some settings for
clinicians – as one way of coping with the patient's behaviour, and the
unwelcome effect on themselves – to use alternative descriptive labels
such as 'cutter', 'slasher' or 'scratcher', often alongside the defensive
reasoning that all such behaviour is merely 'attention seeking'.

Psychoanalytic descriptions and labels such as destructive, narcissistic
or perverse have also been used in connection with cutting and can help
position the behaviour, but again do not necessarily lead to understanding
the meanings behind it for the individual patient. Certainly understanding
the behaviour in terms of direct historical life events carries a certain
validity and indeed attraction, and the link with trauma is explored in this
book. If the behaviour is caused by childhood sexual or physical abuse or
neglect, perhaps we can make sense of it. However, not all those who cut
themselves have experienced obvious past trauma, and this suggests other
dynamics are involved. In recent years psychoanalytic psychotherapy has
tended to move from attributions of cause and direct historical
explanations to an exploration of how the person is in themselves. In this
book I suggest that the origin and meanings of the symptom are to be

found in the internalised processes derived from object relations (cf. Bateman and Holmes 1995). Although this will of course be different for each individual, I am suggesting a particular aspect of early inner object relations, resulting from a combination of the instinctual processes and the environmental that in my experience is common in those attacking their bodies.

This suggestion is central to my exploration of the meaning of self-harm, and is fully illustrated in the more detailed clinical material included later in this book. The development of my understanding of the dynamics involved in self-harm emerged from appreciation of a well-established theoretical concept. This is Glasser's (1992) 'core complex'. In this he describes a universal complex which he places as central to the structure of the psyche. In summary, it has a number of elements, which are outlined here in detail using Glasser's sequence and descriptive terms.

1   The first is the fantasy of *fusion* with the idealised mother who satisfies the person's (originally the infant's) basic need and longing for security. Glasser describes this as the fantasy of ultimate narcissistic fulfilment, or the fantasy of primary narcissism.

2   However, the mother is a split figure, for she is also envisaged as relating entirely narcissistically to the subject, and seen as being both (a) *avaricious* – so that the fusion involves incorporation with a mother who threatens to annihilate the self – this emerges in ideas of engulfment, possession, intrusion and so on; and also (b) *indifferent* – paying insufficient attention or not understanding the emotional needs of the subject – which is always experienced as rejection.

3   This configuration results in *annihilation anxiety*, and concurrent defensive responses characterised by (a) (*narcissistic*) *withdrawal* to a place of safety and self-sufficiency, but this results in worries about being abandoned and falling apart with associated states of depression, isolation and low self-esteem, and this in turn leads to the need again for fusion (as Glasser points out, this part of the core complex is a vicious circle); and (b) (*self-preservative*) *aggression* which aims to destroy or neutralise the powerful, annihilatory mother and of course leads to fears about her loss or rejection.

4   The mother's indifference leads to a similar defensive outcome, of the (a) (*narcissistic*) *withdrawal* from the painful situation, and (b) (*self-preservative*) *aggression* which wants to destroy the unfor-givingness of the mother.

5 Since these responses are concurrent, the *aggression is also turned on to the self.*

(Glasser's emphasis and outline (1992: 496))

Such a universal core complex pervades and influences the whole psyche. It is recognised as common to us all, and as Glasser writes, we all find different 'solutions' to these unavoidable core complex problems. When Glasser first formulated it (1979) and in a later paper (1986), he did not make such wide-ranging claims. However in 1992 he wrote, the solutions 'play a significant role in the aetiology of different pathological conditions as well as, optimally, normality' (1992: 496). At an obvious and superficial level we can experience it with someone we thought we wanted to be with, but we subsequently find ourselves withdrawing as they threaten to become either physically or emotionally over-intrusive – we speak of someone intruding into our personal space. In relationships there can be a longing to make a commitment, yet this can turn into a reluctance to lose a sense of autonomy alongside a fear of feeling rejected if the relationship finishes or the loved person becomes indifferent. In therapy, the core complex can be detected in the very detail of a session. The longing is for the therapist to be close and understand everything, but this leads to a terror of being taken over and suffocated by the intensity of it all and a concomitant anxiety about the therapist's indifference and rejection. How psychic closeness and distance in object relations is experienced and negotiated is a central theme in analytic literature, and pertinent to all those seen in psychotherapy.

In those who are cutting themselves there is clearly this unconscious conflict about psychic distance and closeness, but I am suggesting that there is also a particular configuration involved. This has some similarities with the core complex but is also different from it in significant ways. Most importantly in the psychic conflict that I highlight, the fusion is *not* with an idealised and disappointing mother, although there are strong links with that desire. Instead the fantasy involves being stuck with the malevolent figure of the avaricious, overwhelming mother. This is a development from early infancy and early internalised object relations, whereby the self is captivated and held in thrall by the particular aspect of the mother that threatens complete incorporation. This then forms into a tyrannical inner object configuration who both overwhelms, and from whom there is ambivalence about separation. The fear of being possessed therefore conflicts with the fear of rejection. As with Glasser's core complex, there is the longing to want and have this object, and at the same time to retreat and withdraw from it. There is then a desperate oscillation between going towards and away from the malevolent object. Again the intrapsychic struggle is between opposing forces, but the struggle involves a different configuration, with a different quality and texture.

The psychotherapy with the patients who were cutting revealed this intrapsychic struggle, characterised both by a quality of enslavement and a longing to cut the ties that so tightly bound this relationship. The patients appeared stuck and imprisoned in an enclave, where they were dominated by conflicting desires. It was as if the cutting represented both the marks of the bondage, and the signs of the desire to cut loose and break free. A further characteristic of this psychic conflict was that the young women appeared to be almost enthralled with this stuck state of mind. This has led me to term the internal formation that I am suggesting 'the encaptive conflict'. 'Encaptive' is a word not in current use, but which means to make into a captive – to enthral. It means a state of being captivated, and it also includes a sense of omnipotence and aggression. The encaptive conflict can therefore be seen as a variant and possibly perverse side formation from the core complex. The conflict is unconscious – the action of cutting involves no thinking, rather it is a reaction to bodily sensation and discomfort.

Time after time my experience with the young women in psycho-therapy was that their cutting behaviour demonstrated that what they experienced was felt as an apparently irreconcilable psychic conflict. I am proposing that this involved the specific type of internalised object relationship characterised both by intense involvement/possession and the wish to get away. The only apparent solution to the conflict found and available to those seen seemed to be withdrawal and then aggression turned against the self.

Aspects of the processes derived from inner object relations emerged during the psychotherapy with the young women. The dynamics of the encaptive conflict were projected through the transference relationship, and as therapist I was given a sense of the complex interactions involved. It was through consideration of the psychodynamics that the individual meanings of the encaptive conflict and therefore the cutting could be explored. In general, it seemed that a growing awareness and recognition in the young women that there was more than one feeling involved – love and hate – was needed in order to reconcile the psychic conflict; in other words, both aspects of what was an unconscious conflict had to emerge into conscious awareness.

One can speculate on how actual parental handling, including the mother–daughter relationship, and specific environmental trauma such as sexual or physical abuse, may have contributed to such a constellation in the self, and these issues are explored in this book. However, my contention is that although direct specific trauma might compound this psychic conflict, or indeed act as a trigger for its emergence, the structure and intrapsychic formation were established in infancy.

Alongside these internalised object relations there are obviously powerful instinctual processes involved in self-harm. These are processes which have been affected by and linked experientially to the maternal environment and early parental handling. For example, how the baby learns to handle her instinctual drives and needs emerges from her experience with the external mother and environment. The terribly destructive nature of cutting suggests that the instinctual aggressive drives are in some way out of balance, possibly through excessive stimulation or mismanagement in infancy or childhood. This issue is explored in this book, partly in the context of self-harm as also being a manifestation of the death instinct and destructive processes, initially written about by Freud and looked at in detail in Chapter 2. Sexual instinctual processes are heightened during adolescence as is narcissism, and there is a clear link between adolescent states of mind and self-harm which is discussed later in detail. The theoretical ideas of the development of the body ego, and the sense of the body as other and alien, often because of a sense of dislocation or dissociation, are important aspects of cutting, and this too is heightened especially among young women.

In this book various aspects of attacking the body are discussed, but my contention is that the internal formation of the encaptive conflict could become a useful concept in the psychotherapeutic thinking about self-harm. One theoretical concept that does clearly apply to those who are harming themselves is repetition compulsion, and this is examined in some detail alongside work on addictive behaviours. The difficulty in linking affective sensations to thoughts is central throughout this exploration, and here I have turned in several chapters to Fonagy's (1991) work on the capacity to mentalise – to put sensations and feelings into words.

Chapter 2 begins with the conscious reasons for cutting, before moving on to the unconscious motivation. The need to cut is usually triggered by an immediate anxiety or rejection, but many of the young women wanted to link the reasons for cutting to events that had happened to them in their families, and to past trauma. The person harming herself might not be able to connect sensations with words and might be in a dissociated state. The action of cutting is used to regain a sense of herself, or a 'real' feeling. Undoubtedly many of those who were cutting themselves had histories and early childhood experiences that included loss, abandonment, abuse and neglect. It seemed as if the cutting functioned as a way of excising the pain, or as a way the patient could 'let rip' and so on. None the less, as a gesture the symptom of harming oneself is paradoxical, in that the damage inflicted signifies a desire to continue to live and get on with life. Another theme in this chapter is the use of the implements as a parody of the analytic concept of transitional object. The significance of the use of skin as a medium and surface for communication of conflict is raised. Attacking the body in this controlled manner can function as a way of dealing with what feels uncontrollable, and there can be pleasurable feelings attached to the destruction. As most people involved in this work will recognise, harming can have an addictive quality. There is both a fascination and a masturbatory aspect which includes, like all masturbation, self-soothing and self-healing qualities.

In Chapter 3, I look at the violence of the attack. My thinking is focused on aspects of the processes derived from object relationships that lead to this conflict, involving enslavement and the desire to cut the ties that bind. The encaptive conflict is discussed as comprising both masochism and mastery, and the interplay between the two. Here the contribution of sexual and physical abuse compounding or acting as a trigger to the constellation is explored. Part of the dynamic re-created in the violence of the self-harm concerns an internalised aspect that seems in part to be a re-enactment of an earlier interpsychic dyad. How is physical and sexual abuse internalised by the child? It appears that self-harm replicates the way the trauma is internalised partly in such a 'concrete' form, and also the way the dynamics between abuser and abused are experienced and internalised into an intrapsychic formation. Issues about power, mastery and control are central. There is sometimes a powerful need for the young woman to punish herself for her anger and her sexuality, and this, too, is explored.

Chapter 4 is about the characteristics of an adolescent state of mind and the link between these and self-harm. Common to both the behaviour and the adolescent mind-set are narcissism, aggression, hypersensitivity, a fear of and a focus on death, and a tendency to impulsive action. Cultural and gender aspects are discussed alongside the analytic understanding of an adolescent state of mind. There is an obvious preoccupation with sexuality and separation–individuation issues. This includes the adolescent girl's experiences of her body as something 'other' – something that can be done to and so controlled. This might counteract the power of the uncontrollable physical and emotional changes. Separation from home, and especially from mother, can be problematic, and evokes huge conflicts. Here the fundamental constellation can be seen to include an internalised engulfing mother from whom it feels both desirous and yet impossible to break free. Cutting unconsciously serves to attack the inner mother who crosses all body boundaries, and who is both needed and reviled. Abandonment is a key aspect in assessing later predisposing factors in self-harm, as is neglect and lack of self-care. In this sense self-harm is an acting out founded on the projective identification of the confusion and ambivalence of the psychic conflict. This is heightened during adolescence.

Clinical issues are discussed in Chapters 5 and 6. In Chapter 5 these range from the pragmatic to do with the setting, confidentiality and length of treatment, to more complex concerns such as interpreting the unconscious through dream material, and working with silence. I also explore characteristics of the deepening analytic process, the move to reflection and working with metaphor. In Chapter 6, the details of the psychodynamics of transference and countertransference are discussed, and the powerful impact of projective identification explored. In both these chapters quite detailed clinical material is used. Several years have elapsed since the ending of the work described, and all identifying details have been changed so as to protect the identity of the young women. In some of the descriptions, external events and interactions have been altered or combined to avoid any recognition. I am grateful to one of the patients, whom I have called 'Anne', not only for allowing me to share some aspects of our work but for contributing, as every patient does, so much to my thinking and understanding. In the final section of Chapter 6, the idea of the therapist as a 'new' object is raised.

Chapter 7 widens the exploration of the meanings behind cutting to include social and cultural aspects, and my thinking moves outside the confines of the consulting room and away from the personal psyche. Attacking the surface of the body has taken place over the centuries, and there are fascinating examples of initiation rituals and physical sacrifices from anthropological and archaeological data. Religious practices have included marking the flesh as a route to salvation. Contemporary body piercing and tattooing are acceptable social practices, and can signal membership of a particular group with a particular status. Cutting is part of our cultural heritage with meanings linked to initiation, healing, appeasement and purification. Knowing about the cultural tradition may not help the person who is self-harming, but it can help the therapist by locating the symptom within a wider context. This material raises the question whether there are any meanings that can link contemporary self-harming with earlier or more accepted forms of attacking the body. Some ideas are presented and hypotheses raised. In Chapter 8, the final chapter, the different ideas and meanings are brought together and discussed, and possible models for thinking about self-harm are suggested.

The process of listening to, working with and reading about young women who are attacking their bodies has been a powerful, humbling and salutary experience. It is from this that my thinking about self-harm has emerged. Trying to avoid dogma and routine interpretive stances, a space can be found to think about such experiences and what we make of them. It is with this attitude that I have approached writing this book – a book which hopefully will be both thought provoking and clinically helpful for all those involved with people who attack their own bodies.

Chapter 2

Meanings – conscious reasoning and unconscious motivation

Women's and girls' understanding of their need to harm themselves

Generally, people who deliberately hurt themselves do so because they feel that they need to, and that the act itself makes them feel better for a while and more able to cope. People report overwhelming feelings of misery, emotional distress and hopelessness which lead them to the apparent solution of inflicting pain on their bodies. For some people who harm themselves the solution is felt to be the answer, but for friends, relatives and professionals the solution becomes the problem. To those who are self-harming, cutting serves as a way of owning and controlling the body, and seems to be a solution for those cutting to emotional upset. In situations where a young woman who cuts herself feels overwhelmed or upset by others, and by her own complicated and apparently uncontrollable needs, she can turn and attack her body, and through her aggressive action find some comfort and relief. Through these actions emotional pain becomes physical pain, and therefore easier to deal with, and the metaphorical distinction between body and self is diffused.

Anne, who was referred to the clinic for intensive psychotherapy, spoke of feeling very tense and anxious much of the time. She said this was because she kept thinking about things that had happened to her either recently or in the past. All of a sudden, images, flashbacks and feelings from the past filled her mind. For her, relief came and the tension eased once she had cut herself. She said that she felt quite sure she could not survive without cutting herself. When she cut open her skin, the pain meant that she had something else to think about, and the practical problem of her bleeding arms to deal with. She also spoke of hating her body and herself, and actively hurting herself seemed one way of coping with these feelings. When Anne said to me early in the therapy: 'Don't try and stop me cutting, I'll die if I can't cut', she summarised the strength of the encaptive conflict, although it was several years before I gained a true sense of the constituent aspects involved.

My experience with the young women seen for psychoanalytic psychotherapy was that they tended to focus on the cutting as a way of dealing with an immediate difficult feeling or anxiety. The trigger was often a row within the family or with a friend which contained the threat of abandonment. For example, falling out with a friend, a hostile remark by a teacher, apparent rejection by a parent, were frequently given as the precipitant for the attack. Behind this immediate event there seemed to lie both anxiety about the young woman's fear of destroying the person because of her unexpressed and usually repressed anger, alongside the loss of any hope of having her needs met and gratified by them. The trigger could then be seen to have some sort of link back or echo of the oscillation between opposing psychic forces of having and wanting to be rid of. It was as if the act of self-harm represented something simultaneously profoundly destructive and needy in the mind that broke through and formed the action.

The young women tended to develop their own sequence of events leading to the action, with feelings of indignation and slight that 'justified' what they had done. A few were reluctant to think any further beyond 'this is something I do' and 'this is something I need to do to feel better', and were worried that by coming to the clinic people would try and stop them. Some had a sense that there were more complex reasons that might be contributing to their need to harm themselves, and quickly linked their feelings to upsetting events in their childhood. For many, difficult experiences in childhood had been followed by a disturbing adolescence, and these early experiences, and the angry and upset feelings about them, seemed to underlie their self-destructive behaviour. In my experience some of the young people did find therapeutic value in understanding the origins of their actions, while the more disturbed were unable to make use of such insights. They were struggling to deal with unpredictable sensations, and barely managing the uncontrollable force of emotion.

Over time, many of the patients were able to express their feelings about these experiences in psychotherapy, and most eventually realised there was a link between earlier distress and later symptomatology. Some had experienced serious trauma, while for others there were no obvious reasons for their distress. Out of the fifteen young women who were referred with deliberate self-harm, four had been sexually abused; eight were from families where there had been separation and divorce, often with very little further contact from the absent parent; four had been left by their mothers and four by their fathers. Another was adopted, and felt she had been left both by her mother and father. Four of the young women were at boarding-school and generally felt emotionally neglected or rejected by their families, and three were overly involved with their families and felt under great pressure to be successful. While some had obviously experienced more than one trauma, others felt they were neglected or emotionally abused in a general sense rather than because of a specific trauma.

Lucy was referred at age 18 because of repeated cutting and an overdose attempt. She said she had taken an overdose following a quarrel with a friend who Lucy accused of being too interested in her boyfriend. She had a problematic relationship with her father, who had left the family home when she was a baby, and who now lived and worked abroad. As a child she had spent holidays with him, but had found him bad-tempered, and she had not liked his then girlfriend, and so, from the age of 13, Lucy and her father had had little further contact. In therapy Lucy said she felt confused about her feelings towards her father, and angry and disappointed with her mother who was so critical of him.

Eventually Lucy decided that she would like to see her father again, and we talked about the possibility that she might telephone or write to him, and eventually try to arrange a visit. Consciously hoping for his sympathy and understanding, Lucy decided to tell him immediately on the telephone about her cutting and overdose. Her father dismissed this as 'a lot of nonsense' and Lucy for 'being silly and dramatic'. Lucy was furious and upset by the conversation and afterwards cut her arms badly. In later sessions she was able to think about her strong need to shock her father into responding to her, her anger towards him for his abandonment when she was a baby and his subsequent lack of interest. The cutting was a response to her familiar disappointment in him, and the fear of the strength of her angry and loving feelings towards him. In that sense it was a paradoxical gesture in that she longed to be held safely by him, but her upset at his indifference was represented by the damage to her own arms. By attacking her own body Lucy had wanted to show her parents and friends how angry she was, and how much she had been hurt by them. She also wanted to find out whether her father cared.

The types of difficult life experiences found in the young women attending for psychotherapy are confirmed by a Bristol survey in 1995 where most of the adult women who responded (62 per cent) believed that childhood experiences alone had led them to self-injure, and a number felt that both childhood and adult experiences had contributed. When the women were asked about their childhood experiences, most reported multiple forms of abuse and deprivation. The two most common forms were sexual abuse and neglect (49 per cent) in each category. A similar number reported having suffered from emotional abuse, and a quarter from physical abuse. As the authors of the survey point out, there were clear associations between different types of abuse and neglect, so, for example, most of the women who had suffered neglect or emotional abuse also reported physical or sexual abuse. Some had witnessed family violence although they had not been abused themselves. Separation through death or divorce, and parental illness or alcoholism were also significant contributory reasons. Many felt that lack of communication in the family had led to them seeking out harming themselves as a way of expressing their distress. The survey suggested that for some of these women early experiences of abuse and neglect are repeated in adult relationships, and this contributed to their continuing need to injure themselves (Bristol Crisis Service for Women 1995a: 10).

Some analytic findings

A theme of this book is that the underlying meaning of self-harm originates in early childhood experiences – the events that trigger the action have their roots in old patterns and old wounds. Clearly the psychodynamic and psychoanalytic explanations of self-harming behaviour stress the early relationships in a person's life. In particular, they focus on how any traumatic or abusive events are inwardly responded to and taken up into a person's imaginative and fantasy life. In this sense self-harm is basically a symptom expressing disturbance originating from an earlier, prepubertal time, though for reasons explored in Chapter 4 it often emerges during adolescence, and is characterised by an adolescent mind-set. It is as if the attack on the body becomes the only way to communicate deep distress, which, both at the time it was experienced and the time it re-emerges, cannot be put into words.

The psychoanalytic literature highlights loss, separation, abandonment, abuse and neglect as key aspects – findings that confirm the experiences of the young women in the study. The central themes in the analytic literature on the sexual and aggressive elements – self-harm as a self-destructive impulse, namely an attack on part of the body serving as a substitute for the whole; and the hatred and confusion towards the sexual body – are explored in depth in Chapters 3 and 4. In this chapter my central schema is the idea that attacking the body is a paradoxical gesture which emerges in a number of ways, including the ritual use of implements, and the skin as a medium for communication.

An overall and not unexpected finding in the analytic literature is that inadequate or disruptive early object relationships are seen as a central contributory factor to self-harm, and such experiences are reflected in later difficulties with forming close attachments and meaningful relationships. The infantile experiences with the environment are internalised, and, as inner object relations, affect later relationships – including the transference relationship as it emerges in the psychotherapy. The regressive quality in relationships is generally acknowledged, as if the person is continually in touch with the need to satisfy earlier deficiencies. This links with another common finding which is a narcissistic orientation in the person who is attacking her body, and the auto-erotic aspects of the act are also recognised. It is generally agreed that traumatic events such as neglect, and physical and sexual abuse, are linked with the later need to harm oneself, and can lead to basic alterations in the experience of the body, and the internalisation of early negative caretaking processes and negative attachment. The few specific studies on young people suggest that they are caught up in complex struggles around issues of separation, individuation and differentiation, exacerbated by inadequacies in their early attachments. I shall now look at some of the more useful studies that focus on the reasons for self-harm. These analytic studies tend to be based on a small number of patients, or on treatment with one individual.

One of the most valuable collection of papers comes from a symposium on self-mutilation and self-cutting in the late 1960s (Burnham 1969; Kafka 1969; Pao 1969; Podvoll 1969), where the findings outlined above were emphasised. In his paper, Podvoll (1969) writes of the loneliness of the act, performed alone, on the person's own body and shared with no one. It takes place at a time when the person feels most detached and removed from others, and involves a splitting phenomenon. He emphasises three dynamics. The first is the 'flight from deeply dependent, even symbiotic wishes toward a more primitive love object to a reliance on the auto-erotic use of one's own body' – in other words, a reactive move from dependency on another to separation and increased self-sufficiency. The second is a 'capacity to treat one's own flesh with scorn and contempt necessary to allay more narcissistic urges' – in other words, hatred of the body; the third is the diversion by the patient of aggression on to herself 'a fixed and seemingly indestructible object, in this way the patient manages to preserve intact her split off and idealized object'. Here, aggression turned inwards is safer than the possibly destructive aspects of what may feel like uncontrollable aggression towards another (1969: 220).

Pao's paper (1969) focuses on young female hospitalised 'cutters', who in his view seemed to vacillate between being psychotic and being 'normal'. Each young woman also had other symptoms, such as eating disorders, other ways of harming themselves and suicidal thoughts. The symptoms had emerged between the ages of 12 and 14, and had led to outpatient treatment and eventually to several hospitalisations. These patients' developmental histories revealed that the mother had played a central part in the family system, in contrast to the father who tended to stay on the periphery. However during infancy there appeared to be a lack of maternal handling, or frequent changes in the quality or quantity of maternal care due to circumstances such as mother's illness, other siblings or a poor relationship between the parents. Pao reports that the patients were fearful of their own aggression, and expressed repugnance towards female sexuality. They were often socially isolated and had problems sustaining same-sex relationships.

An interesting observation is that Pao found that, at the time of cutting, his patients were in an altered ego state where they became self-engrossed, unaware of their surroundings and auto-erotic in the sense of being totally unrelated to anyone else at that moment. He describes it as 'a regressed ego state with surrendering of autonomous ego functioning to a drive-dominated act which was simultaneously sadistic and masochistic' (1969: 198). While consciousness was suspended the patient was able to retain physical control, and was able to remember what she had done. This state of mind has similarities to the experience of depersonalisation and derealisation, but, as Pao reminds us, in depersonalisation the person's sense of their participation in the action is lessened although they are highly self-aware, while in cutting the reverse is the case. In other words, the young women were very involved in the immediate experience, but had little if any self-awareness at that moment. In the clinical material he describes, both patients cut themselves when aggressive feelings arose over loss and separation. Sometimes this was an actual separation (for example, when the therapist went away on holiday), while at other times the patients engineered a separation (for example, leaving the hospital ward). This finding leads Pao to suggest that as early as possible in the treatment the patient's difficulties over separation and abandonment need to be dealt with, even though this carries the risk of further cutting. The therapist in the early stages of the treatment has the responsibility for making connections until the patient progresses to a stage where she can make such links herself.

In both of these papers Podvoll and Pao are describing dissociation – though they use different terms – which is a concept of great relevance in self-harm. In a dissociated state, where there is an interruption in awareness, a person either feels no pain when she hurts herself, or does it so that she can feel *something*. Dissociation is a specific, adaptive, automatic and dynamic response to severe trauma which separates and isolates the original traumatic experience, so that the central self escapes from the pain and reality of what has happened, and emotional distress is avoided (Gardner forthcoming). If there is a threat of an associated experience the person again emotionally 'cuts off', and ironically uses actual cutting as a way of dealing with what is happening. Worth noting here is the work of Orbach (1994) who found dissociative tendencies a unique factor characteristic of destructive behaviour, as it is a process which restricts both one's sense of one's body and one's experience of the self and world. As I explore later, there is an inability to think about either the trauma or the associated trauma, and, as there can be no symbolic mental representation for what has happened, all this has to be managed in the therapeutic work.

A useful study of adolescent self-harm has been made by Simpson and Porter (1981) who describe their work with twenty young people – sixteen girls and four boys – who were harming themselves, usually by cutting or burning parts of their bodies, and who had been hospitalised. This study has very similar findings to my own study, with the familiar range of harming behaviour and damaging childhood experiences, and the poignant desperation involved in the attacks. Twelve of the young people had also made serious suicide attempts, and another six reported thinking about suicide, but none of them intended to kill themselves by cutting or burning. Most of them abused alcohol and/or drugs. The authors studied variables of physical abuse, sexual abuse and the sense of abandonment and the link with the self-harming behaviour. The findings demonstrated that most, if not all, of the young people had experienced some form of actual disruption in early childhood. One or both parents had left the home, and replacement caretakers were often inadequate. Twelve of the girls and one of the boys had been physically abused by a parent, and nine of the patients referred to inappropriate sexual involvement with a close family member. The authors note the desperate sense of isolation and the feeling that they were unlovable, which was expressed by nearly all the participants. While they searched for relationships, many refused to form meaningful attachments. For the young people, harming themselves appeared to act as a form of physical stimulation almost akin to the physical pain experienced in childhood. It also acted as a focus for aggressive feelings and contained an element of self-punishment, often for sexual feelings and behaviour. Finally the harming was also seen as a non-verbal statement of their despair and a cry for help.

In his paper Daldin (1990) focuses on psychotherapy with a 14-year-old girl, but shares his experience that many patients who inflict injury on themselves are characterised by having a tragic and chaotic life which is dominated by loss and leaves them depressed. He also notes a study with the unusual finding that many patients had experienced early physical trauma or surgery, usually before the age of 6, and that most perceived menstruation as something that made them miserable or that frightened them. Daldin's patient, Chris, had a disrupted and difficult early childhood; her parents' marriage broke down when she was 2, following verbal and physical fighting. Subsequent care of the young children was confused and there were major disruptions. Chris was seen for intensive analytic psychotherapy during the six weeks she was in hospital, and this continued on an outpatient basis. Daldin's account is helpful because he looks in detail at session material. For example, during one session as an outpatient, when Chris reported having cut herself, her associations to this were to her discharge from hospital, and to earlier experiences of being abandoned by her parents. Daldin notes that Chris became increasingly angry and depressed and said she felt 'alone'. Chris pulled a pin from her jacket and stuck it through the skin of her left forearm and then through the skin between her thumb and first finger. She said, 'See, I can stick it in . . . and pull it out . . . and I don't feel a thing' (1990: 285). Daldin interprets her anger as the result of rejection by him because he had discharged her from hospital. He feels that her anger turned into carrying out an action that would force him to readmit her. Chris confirmed this and threw the pin away. Daldin comments later in his discussion that Chris was not able to manage and hold on to her sexual and aggressive feelings as thoughts; rather she felt she had to act them out – on some occasions in the sessions.

The well-known work by the Laufers (1984) can be added to these papers on adolescent breakdown. This provides a valuable conceptual framework. They emphasise the use of the body as the channel for the expression of all the adolescent's feelings and fantasies. Adolescents who have difficulties in forming relationships are especially vulnerable, and are seen as in a state of 'developmental deadlock' where there is no possibility of moving forward into adulthood nor regressing back to dependence. It is as if the only route is via self-destructive action, and the body becomes the site for representation of this. This is explored further in Chapter 4.

Paradoxical gestures

As I have proposed, attacking the body is essentially a paradoxical gesture in that the apparently destructive act reflects a desire to continue to live and get on with life. Cutting can function as a way of cutting off from internal pain by providing a distraction. A further paradox is that for some, the physical pain caused by the action can instil some sort of feeling, in contrast to emotional deadness. As a result of the pain they had inflicted on their bodies, which ironically some of the young women did not experience as pain, these feelings of dissociation left them, and some reported feeling alive again. Some of the patients seen at the clinic spoke of feeling half alive, empty or even unreal before they wounded or poisoned themselves. The feelings of emotional deadness were replaced through self-inflicted physical pain. Some of those who cut or burned themselves felt that they could concentrate on the wound, rather than on their other worries. They felt that hurting themselves had been a solution, a way of releasing tension and coping with problems that enabled them to get on with their lives. For a few of the patients the pain served as some form of punishment, and eased their bad feelings and hatred towards themselves. Another function was that some of the young women felt that the attacks on their bodies helped them to feel in control of themselves, and what they were feeling.

Rosie would burn her arms by pressing a lighted cigarette on her skin until she could hear and smell the burn. Rosie asserted that it was only at that point that she could feel the pain, and in her words 'feel real again'. It was hard for her to explain what she meant by this, but she described often feeling unreal and strange. The experience of self-inflicted burning seemed to force her to reconnect to herself, and she reported feeling in charge and in control once more.

Addiction and fantasies around risk, danger and death

I now turn to an understanding of the repetitive aspect of the behaviour, and highlight the addictive aspects of repeated self-injury. While the initial act of cutting can serve as a form of self-help, by releasing tension or as a way of coping with unbearable feelings, the way in which the act is responded to influences whether the person does it again. In general, repetition seems to be influenced by a number of factors: whether the original circumstances still apply; the person's own beliefs about the action of cutting, hitting or burning her body; her own and others' emotional response to the original act; and good mood changes produced by the action (Holmes 2000). Tantam and Whittaker (1992) usefully suggest two main reasons for this, which may often be combined. The first is that the behaviour can be coercive, in that the self-harming produces a wanted response from others; second, that it is relieving, in that the action produces a lightening of mood, either through biochemical alterations and the associated release of endorphins (the body's own analgesics), or conditioning, or symbolically. I would add two further points, which are that once the threshold has been crossed it is easier to act again; and second, that included in the response is a form of fearful excitement which may never be regained after the first time, but is still longed for.

'The manipulation of the idea of death is not devoid of pleasure' (Haim 1974: 208). Here I want to emphasise as part of the sense of fearful excitement the strong attraction to risk-taking situations among some of the young women I saw. It can be seen as similar to the ambiguous pleasure of playing with fire, with the accompanying risk of burning oneself, a pleasure which includes a strong element of masochism. Attacking the body seemed one way in which these young women dealt with uncertainty and anxiety. The more extreme forms of cutting, burning and hitting led the young person to feel that she could bring death upon herself; that, despite life feeling out of control, she could in fantasy control the time and manner of her own destruction and even death. A further fantasy, perhaps belonging to a younger age, was that while the part feeling the painful and unbearable feelings could be killed off, another, happier part of themselves could then live. Despite feelings of dependence, the person who self-harms can demonstrate her autonomy and ultimate independence by such symbolic actions. Again this is a further paradox, for, in the young woman's belief that she can kill herself, there exists her recognition that she is alive and free, and in that sense no longer a dependent child.

Inevitably the fear of death, and the terror of uncertainty, can lead to a fear of living, or a fear of becoming too attached to life. In the same way that some of the young women had experienced early failures of attachment with their mothers, and later had experienced abusive attachments, they were fearful of any further relationships, including the therapeutic relationship. Some form of deliberately hurting themselves, while reminding the young women that they existed, at the same time restricted their existence and the formation of intimate relationships. The fear of relationships can go together with a realisation that there is a need for intimacy, and part of the self-destruction connects to a wish to annihilate that need.

There is a large body of analytic theory linked to the concept of the death instinct. Freud (1920) first described the death instinct as aiming at destructuralisation, dissolution and death. He saw it as a biological drive to return to the inorganic. Segal has taken this biological concept and emphasises the psychological aspects, seeing it as a drive 'to annihilate the need, to annihilate the perceiving experiencing self, as well as anything that is perceived' (1993: 55). She describes how this often becomes a powerful projection in the countertransference which can lead to feelings of deadness and paralysis in the analyst, or stimulate feelings of aggression and persecution. Sometimes all the life force becomes the responsibility of the analyst, who is left feeling that they are keeping the process, and the patient, alive. The patient may be avoiding the pain caused by the awareness of their need for intimacy with another. This leads to emotional and sometimes actual physical attacks on the self and emotional attacks on the other person, the other person being hated and envied because they are so desperately needed. This is an experience that I found particularly in the work with the most disturbed patients I saw, and is examined in further detail in Chapter 6.

In a seminal paper Joseph (1982) takes the concept of the death instinct, and discusses the libidinal satisfaction linked to self-destruction. Her ideas on this are especially valuable. She particularly discusses the way such difficulties are constituted in people's internal relationships, and therefore might emerge in the transference with an analyst. In a telling passage she pinpoints 'the deeply addictive nature of this type of masochistic constellation and the fascination and hold on them it has' (1982: 450). She also describes the addiction in terms of the patient being 'enthralled' by it, and linked to a mental activity of going over and over something – a process she terms 'chuntering'. This process is the antithesis of thought and development. She writes that such patients have withdrawn into a secret world of violence 'where part of the self has been turned against another part, parts of the body being identified with parts of the offending object, and that this violence has been highly sexualized, masturbatory in nature, and often physically expressed' (1982: 455). The examples she gives are of head-banging, pulling at hair and so on, physical activities that mirror the equivalent verbal chuntering. The addictive quality means that it is hard for the patients to resist, and it acts as 'a constant pull towards despair and near-death so that the patient is fascinated and unconsciously excited by the whole process' (1982: 456). Here I equate this with the sense that I describe of the 'fearful excitement' engendered by the attack.

In the clinical example that follows, Shannon, who was referred initially to the clinic with an eating disorder, veered between dramatic anorexic and bulimic phases. After several admissions to adolescent units where her weight was maintained, Shannon began to drink heavily, experiment excessively with drugs, cut her arms deeply and made several suicide attempts, usually by taking overdoses. On one occasion she climbed out on to the second-storey window-ledge of her mother's home, where she threatened to jump, and involved a number of people in her rescue. Eventually she was 'talked down' by a neighbour. Later, Shannon confided how much she had enjoyed her stays in the units, where she and other residents would talk together for hours about their situations, and the various methods of hurting themselves that they had all tried. It seemed that Shannon needed the drama and excitement of her self-destruction. She could then talk about these events and what she was doing, without allowing herself to think about the reason or meaning that lay behind her behaviour. Her self-harm also served as a way of avoiding relating to her therapist in the transference. No meaningful relationship in the transference was possible, since her dramatic symptoms created a distance between herself and the therapist.

Again there is a paradox here, in that the addictive need for such excitement and the special attention that may result from it is in direct proportion to the lack or absence of the experience of having been treated as a person in their own right. Some of the young women felt they had merely fulfilled parental need, or experienced themselves as extensions of a parent's narcissism. The actions of attacking the body provided them with their own identity, as well as their own form of comfort and way of solving their problems. The entry into the public domain, via an overdose or noticed body injury, gave some of them a chance to be special and different. Yet some who were harming themselves in a serious way seemed to be demanding an authoritative intervention from an adult, powerful enough to balance their own omnipotent ideas of the amount of damage that they could cause to themselves.

Ritual and the implements of self-harm as transitional objects

When the behaviour becomes addictive and is regularly repeated, ceremonial symbolism and ritual around the actual harming may in turn become crucial, or even addictive in their own right. I think that at this point we see elements of magic and superstition entering a process that becomes akin to healing and/or salvation. This hypothesis can best be illustrated with reference to the work with Mary, who is also discussed in a later chapter.

Mary kept her razors in a special wooden box, wrapped in a piece of velvet cloth. The box was kept under her bed. When her mother found out about the cutting, she made Mary hand over the razors. Mary bought some more and hid the box under a loose floorboard in her bedroom. Even when Mary stopped cutting she felt it helped her to know that her secret supply was still safe. Before cutting herself Mary laid out her razors on the cloth, and would choose one for that occasion. She would sometimes play certain music while she made her choice. After the cutting Mary followed a routine with cleaning up the blood and tending to the cuts, before putting on plasters, covering up her arms again, and cleaning and hiding the razor back in its special place. She said that just opening the box made her feel calmer.

Turning to Freud, we see that he terms such responses as 'neurotic ceremonial' (1907: 117), and classes the behaviour alongside obsessional neurosis. His comment is that although such routines and arrangements, which always have to be carried out in the same, or in a methodically varied, manner, give the impression of being mere formalities, and in themselves are meaningless both to the person performing them and to any observer, they cannot be changed. Any deviation from the ceremonial leads to great anxiety – this was certainly true in Mary's experience. My emphasis is that such ritual may consciously have no meaning, but there is both function and meaning at an unconscious level. Freud links the need for such ceremonial back to earlier emotional conflicts, and although the original conflicts are no longer consciously remembered, he believes that the behaviour acts as an insurance or a protection against a sense of guilt and the anxious expectation of punishment. (I discuss this idea of an unconscious sense of guilt more fully in Chapter 3, in the context of the link between abuse and self-harming behaviour.) The symbolic ritual and ceremony around self-harm can be understood at an unconscious level as a protective measure against punishment and damage. Possibly Mary's attention to detail around the act of cutting served as a displacement and a way of avoiding recognising the damage and punishment she was inflicting on herself.

I think the attachment to the implements of self-destruction, such as razors or knives, can be seen as a parody of the usual form of transitional object. Take Winnicott's (1971) idea of the teddy bear or some special object as the first 'not-me' possession and a preparation for separation and weaning, and substitute razors or knives. I think for some of the patients attending for psychotherapy, these became special comforting objects that symbolised their need for safety and security and their capacity to act autonomously. For Mary the razor acted as a perverse transitional object. Among young people heavily involved with drugs, the substances and paraphernalia associated with certain drug use lead to ceremony and ritual, and an attachment to the objects and procedure aside from the effects of the drugs. The razor is an ordinary object in its own right with day-to-day and common associations. In that sense the object is free and available for all the projections that the person will put on to it – it can become a symbol of whatever is longed for.

One of the fantasies projected on to the razor is that it will change something, and possibly make everything better. If there is some change and the young person does feel relieved or altered by her use of the object, then the object itself will become further imbued with transformative properties, and her attachment to it will increase. The object becomes seen as a reliable friend, a constant companion, that can ease pain. It is clear that part of the relief brought by the ritual is that of control. The controlled use of an object such as a razor leads the young person to feel that the object can help her to contain all the chaotic feelings she is experiencing. Some of these conflictual feelings will be linked to sexuality, and in the following section I explore the actual bodily attacks as a reflection of aspects of auto-eroticism.

Auto-eroticism

In this context Hopper's work on drug addiction is illuminating, especially his idea that the addiction to drugs, or in this context attacking the body, is primarily an addiction to certain fantasies and compulsions that are linked and helped by the action (1995: 1129). He believes that by using the drugs the addict is able to avoid the anxieties associated with the fantasies and compulsions. In other words, the drug-taking displaces the anxiety of certain types of fantasy, especially those that evoke feelings of shame and guilt. Central are those fantasies involving sexual identity and feelings. I want to take his idea and transpose it to repeated cutting and look at the behaviour as a way of dealing with conflictual feelings over sexuality. This is a central theme in Chapter 4 on predisposing factors, but it is worth raising in the context of the repetitive behaviour which in itself suggests some sort of masturbatory quality. I have already mentioned the idea of the enthralment or fearful excitement evoked by direct attacks on the body, which does appear to link to a form of auto-eroticism. It is worth remembering here that Welldon (1988) uses the word 'perverse' to refer to self-harm, which she sees as a pathological manifestation of women acting as if their whole body were a sexual organ.

A quick word about definitions: in this context the term 'masturbation' is used in this context to cover all forms of self-stimulation, involving any part of the body, and as a part of the ritualised damaging of the body. The term 'auto-erotic' is used in the general sense of a type of sexual behaviour in which the person gains satisfaction from the use of their own body, and no other person is needed. This obviously links to narcissistic disorder which can be understood as an inability to really love and value oneself, and therefore the inability to love someone else.

As discussed above, there is a sense that some patients may become enthralled by their own capacity to destroy themselves, and associated with this has to be a form of sexual excitement and masochistic pleasure. Hopper (1995) reminds us that masturbation is one of the earliest forms of self-healing and self-soothing. 'It offers opportunities for withdrawal into a sense of safety afforded by the isolation of a protective narcissistic bubble' (1995: 1134). Hopper goes on to explain how fantasies associated with masturbation, or masturbatory type behaviour, can help make sense of a traumatic experience and can often be traced back to very early memories. Such early trauma may involve some sort of failure in early object relations between the mother and baby. Whatever the reason and circumstances of this failure, the baby internalises the experience, defends herself against the trauma and grows into a child who cannot place her trust in others, and who also has very strong destructive impulses.

This next clinical vignette illustrates the experience of such lack of trust. Amy expected nothing good to come from the outside world – none of her earlier experiences led her to expect otherwise. She was terrified of and hated relating to people. Perhaps to protect herself from painful memories she felt a deep antagonism to self-knowledge. Amy was given up for adoption by her teenage mother. It was not possible for the right placement to be found immediately, so for the first six months of her life she was fostered by two different families. Amy told me that there had been difficulties with the first foster family who had lots of problems, and apparently she had not been looked after properly. The adoptive family chosen for Amy seemed also to have had difficulties looking after her, and from the age of 11 Amy was placed in boarding-school. She was expelled from two schools, and moved to a third in her GCSE year. It was at this point that Amy was referred both for cutting herself and an attempted suicide through taking an overdose.

When Amy first came to sessions she was silent and looked very sullen. She was quite overweight and also had a serious skin condition with acne on her chest, face and back. When I tried to encourage her to speak or suggested what might be happening between us, Amy appeared not to hear me. She felt that the sessions were pointless, and eventually said that she saw me as another social worker who would make all decisions for her and not take any notice of what she wanted or said. It seemed that her expectation was that meeting with me for therapy would replicate her early infancy, and be experienced by her as punishing and non-nurturing. However, Amy continued to attend, mainly because she was regularly brought by someone from her boarding-school. It seemed that she was willing enough to come to the sessions, but at this stage was psychologically unable to take part in a relationship with me.

Amy gave me a strong sense of her mistrust and hostility. Over time she began to tell me about how awful she felt about her looks – she felt huge on the outside, misshapen, and her spots made everything seem much worse. Amy longed to have a boyfriend, but did not feel that she would meet anyone who would love her or who she could like. Over the months Amy began to speak about how difficult it was to make friends, and how, when she did, something happened to make it all go wrong, and the friendship broke up. Amy would brood about what had happened, going over and over every detail of how unfair it all was, and how horrible people were to her.

I gathered that when things went wrong, Amy would hide away somewhere on the school grounds, take out a razor from her collection, and carefully cut her arms and stomach. She told me she liked doing it, because she liked the feeling of the warm blood trickling down her skin, and the patterns she could make. At times like that Amy said that she felt very alone, but safe because there was just her. Amy had many unexpressed feelings about her natural mother, but she did say that she would like to have a baby which she would keep and love; on the other hand she was terrified that at some time she might become pregnant and so be like this sexual, all-powerful and rejecting mother. This internalised sexual, all-powerful yet rejecting mother formed part of the encaptive conflict. Amy was captivated by this constellation but longed to be rid of it, as she too had been got rid of. Amy quite liked her adoptive parents, but said how anxious her adoptive mother was all the time. Amy felt that she could not tell her anything as this caused more worry, while her adoptive father appeared to her to be a remote and rather unpredictable man.

When Amy felt rejected by a friend she comforted herself by cutting her skin. This seemed to her a private special thing that she did to herself, which both excited and reassured her. The ritual around the cutting and the smearing of blood on her stomach and arms served as a displacement for her anxieties about relationships which always went wrong. This anxiety appeared to lead back to her earliest relationships, the rejection by her birth mother and the neglect in her first foster family. It seemed to me that there was a connection between the material that Amy brought about wanting a baby, and the cutting and smearing blood on her stomach. I thought that the actions were some sort of metaphoric representation in that she had fantasies about being pregnant, but the experience of being rejected was so strong that she needed to enact the anger and destruction on her own womb. I think that for Amy the stimulation and pain to her skin caused feelings of excitement and comfort. It was also something that she could rely on and do for herself – in that sense her behaviour was a form of masturbation. Over time Amy was able to speak a little bit about her past, but generally she found that it was too difficult to think about it and to manage the painful feelings she experienced.

Following an altercation with a teacher after bringing alcohol into school, Amy took an overdose and was asked to leave. She returned home. We continued our relationship by letter, and Amy reported that she felt better at home, and was surprised to find that she could talk a bit more to her mother. Amy found a job working as a nanny for a family friend who had two little girls, and she wrote that she enjoyed this. She sent me photos of the little girls in the bath, and of herself to show me that she had lost some weight and that her acne had improved with drug treatment. When I last heard from Amy she had enrolled on a health and beauty course, although of course her early experiences remained unresolved, and her deep suspicions about relationships had been only slightly alleviated.

The skin as a medium for communication

In behaviour such as cutting, burning and hitting, the skin is directly damaged, and this is symbolically meaningful. After all, our skin acts as a container for our sense of self and the most primitive parts of our personality, and is also a boundary between ourselves and others, and what is inside and outside ourselves. It is the border or the edge between our inner selves and the social world. It acts as a membrane that protects us, but is also the actual surface of what we present to the outside world. The skin can conceal but also demonstrate. Given this understanding, skin can be seen as the surface where feelings that are not verbalised are sometimes expressed. In other words, the body and the skin that surrounds it show other people and ourselves what we are. Through awareness of our body we understand that we are alive and have a self. Both body and skin, and what we do to them, can be seen as the locus for our anxieties about being alive including our fears of falling apart, and the differentiation between ourselves and others.

There has been much analytic thought about skin and its function. Pines (1993), for example, explores the relationship between the baby and mother as expressed through touching the skin. Clearly the way a mother touches her baby reveals a wide range of feelings, including tenderness and disgust. The infant will respond – sometimes through her skin, and feelings that cannot be spoken about are sometimes expressed through a sore or irritated skin condition. The mother serves, if she can, as a containing object for the baby's distress, and as Bick (1968) writes in her well-known paper, is experienced concretely as a skin. The mother's successful capacity to do this results in the baby's introjection of the experience of feeling contained. In Britton's formulations, if the mothering person is receptive and capable, she can make sense of the infant's experience and transform a bodily sensation (Beta elements) into 'something more mental, which could be used for thought or stored as memory' (Alpha elements) (Britton 1991: 105). If this process of introjection is faulty or inadequate, the baby may develop a 'second-skin' formation where the baby's dependence on the mother to contain the distress is replaced by a pseudo-independence; this leads to a 'general fragility in later integration' and 'manifests itself in states of unintegration . . . as either partial or total type of muscular shell or a corresponding verbal muscularity' (Bick 1968: 485). This quality is one that I recognised in several of the more disturbed patients seen for psychotherapy at the clinic. At its best, the analytic environment can at times function as a mental skin for patients unused to containing strong emotional experiences. If the psychotherapist is receptive to certain emotional somatic experiences in the patient, these can be processed and transformed by words into a mental experience that is then thought about.

Interestingly, Kafka's (1969) work with a patient who cut herself and sometimes swallowed pills indiscriminately provides clinical material that focuses on the issues discussed above, including the patient's use of her body (rather than razor) as a transitional object and her narcissistic and erotic approach to her surface skin. The young woman's parents were separated, but there were intimations of an overly involved and erotic relationship with her mother. Difficulties around touching and skin sensitivity related back to the patient's infancy, when the little girl suffered from a generalised dermatitis which had led to almost her entire body having to be bandaged for the first year of her life. Although hungry for contact, the parents recalled the acute pain for the baby as a result of that contact. Furry pets and dolls played a central part in the family, and seemed to link to the importance of texture and touching later in her adolescence. In his analysis Kafka links the symptom to the early skin disorder, and feels that the patient did treat parts of the surface of her body as though she were not dealing with quite living skin. He writes: 'she was very much preoccupied with the, for her, very much *unfinished business* of establishing her body scheme' (Kafka 1969: 211).

The skin can become the channel for the communication of pre-verbal feelings and feelings that cannot be expressed. In some of the patients seen for psychotherapy the wounds on their skin served as symbolic scars representing their earlier history, and once the cutting became public it appeared as a desperate attempt to communicate and tell this story. Earlier memories of past traumas are remembered through the body and bodily sensations, though they are not necessarily consciously accessible (Scott 1998a). The young women I saw were unable to find a way to speak. Instead they had to act through bodily sensations, and to represent their feelings through their actions. As Scott notes elsewhere, 'the body is both the site of the traumatic event and the site of memory, and has to do the work of a "monument" . . . at the same time as the subject lives her life' (1998b: 4). Although the body is often silent, when the skin is ruptured through an attack, the wound becomes the route of remembrance.

In this way self-harm is a statement about the self, but one that is expressed through the attack on the body. External events and the way they have become internalised and fantasised are registered and noted through self-destruction. Here we have the intriguing connection between surface and depth. What is shown through appearance following cutting is linked to the inner conflict and the self of the person. In that sense the deep inner trauma is made visible on the surface of the body. Internal objects and the experiences of them are projected outside and then identified with on the skin surface. The opening up of the skin is an explicit opening up of the boundary of the body, and an implicit opening up of the self. However, the action is ambiguous in that frequently it is private, secret and covered up. The scars and wounds may 'speak', but there is often no one to listen, and no reply is asked for. It is only when the attack is uncovered that the opening up can be acknowledged and becomes public, and there is often intense ambivalence about the discovery and ensuing dialogue.

There is an opportunity for the scars to speak and get a reply in the psychotherapeutic relationship. In other words, the attack on the body can then lead to a relationship and so become a transformative action. Theoretically the establishment of a containing space, a type of mental skin or boundary where ideas can be held, allows the process of thinking to become established, so that over time the capacity for self-knowledge can be developed. The idea of the psychotherapeutic relationship acting as a second skin allows for the release of the pressure on the person's actual skin, and attacks on the therapy can be held and dealt with by the psychotherapist.

Chapter 3

Turning the anger inwards
Masochism and mastery

This chapter is about the terribly destructive nature of cutting, and the way aggressive instinctual processes are affected and linked with both the early parental environment and later traumatic experiences. In the first chapter, Glasser's (1992) core complex was outlined: briefly summarised as the fantasy of fusion leading to annihilation anxiety; the concurrent defensive responses from that, and also from the fear of the mother's indifference; both these defensive responses leading to aggression turned inwards against the self, and enacted on the surface of the body. The encaptive conflict that I suggest as a central unconscious psychic formation among the young women seen for psychotherapy who were self-harming is a variant and possibly perverse side formation of this core complex. In this context, it is interesting to note that Glasser's (1979) original concept was seen in the context of perversion. However, instead of fusion with an idealised mother, the encaptive conflict involves the captivation by an avaricious object who overwhelms, and from whom there is ambivalence about separation. The fear of being possessed conflicts with the fear of rejection, and the psychic conflict leads to a defensive compromise. The solution to the conflict is hostility, which is turned inwards against the self and the body, rather than directed outwards on to an external object.

Writing about aggression and violence, Glasser (1998) refers to conscious, intentional action involving the actual assault on the body of one person by another. He separates out self-preservative violence and sado-masochistic violence. In the former type the aim is to negate danger, while in sadism the aim is to inflict pain and suffering. For the young women who were cutting, the attacks seemed to involve a combination of both these types of aggression. Instead of attacking another person, the young woman turned her violent action against her own body, but *as if* attacking another person, or a separate part of herself. It seemed that her body was at that point both connected and dislocated from her sense of self. At an unconscious level her body, or part of her body, felt owned and possessed by an all-powerful 'other'. The patients hurt themselves to ward off the dangerous thoughts evoked by the partial emergence of the sensations linked to the encaptive conflict.

In both cases of aggression – towards other people and the self – the underlying motive is the same: 'a wish to attack *thoughts*, in oneself or in another' (Fonagy 1995: 582). So what are the terrible thoughts that need to be attacked and kept at bay at all costs? The thoughts are those resulting from uncomfortable sensations and frightening or anxious feelings. This discomfort originates from processes derived from early object relations. In addition, it may include how experiences of specific trauma, such as physical and sexual abuse, have been taken up, internalised and so managed. The encaptive conflict is a formation involving a tyrannical inner object configuration which both overwhelms, and from which there is ambivalence about separation. The fear of being possessed conflicts with the fear of rejection. In those who are harming themselves it involves the earliest experiences of object relations, and how these are remembered and structured. This structure can be compounded by direct trauma or cumulative traumatic events. Alternatively the encaptive conflict can be triggered and activated by specific trauma, which then provide the impetus for its emergence. The process is intrapsychic, it has become an inner object relationship, although it originated as an interpsychic relationship. The wounds from cutting can be seen as a metaphoric representation of the encaptive conflict, suggesting both the marks of enslavement and the desire to cut free. In that sense the symptom can be seen as evidence of the return of the repressed, and a statement about the self and what has happened.

Self-harm is a registering of the dynamics of an inner object formation, a form of mapping on the body, and an embodiment of the related mental phenomena. It is in part an enactment, founded on projective identification of unintegrated feelings from these earlier experiences and trauma. What is felt initially and internally as a sensation is externalised and fixed as memory on the skin. Paradoxically, cutting is both a defence against thinking about the past, and the evocation of sensations of an earlier violation in another form. As a noticeable proportion of the patients seen for psychotherapy had been abused during childhood, the specific link between this and cutting is explored in the next part of this chapter.

The dynamics of abuse and the link with self-harm

Clinical recognition over the past twenty years of the long-term effects both of child sexual abuse and physical abuse has emerged from findings linking later mental illness in women with these earlier assaults. In general, those who report abuse are more likely than those who do not to experience symptoms of depression, emotional problems and suicidal ideas or attempts. They also report feelings of low self-esteem, alienation, distrust, sexual acting out or sexual difficulties, and self-harm. Other long-term effects may include eating disorders and induced obesity. Some children cope with abuse by dissociation, or attributing the sensations experienced to another child or to another part of themselves, while others repress the memory or try to block it out from their conscious memory. Even if the dissociation seems successful, the underlying distress will usually re-emerge in some form of symptomatology, or later as a recovered memory. The effects vary according to the age of the child, the life circumstances, the frequency of the abuse and the degree of aggression and physical damage involved (Gardner 1990).

An important study by Van der Kolk *et al.* (1991) demonstrated that early histories of physical and sexual abuse, as well as parental neglect and separation, were strongly linked with later acts of deliberate self-injury. De Young (1982) found that 58 per cent of the forty-five sexually abused women and girls whom she interviewed injured themselves by cutting, burning, attempts to break bones or self-poisoning. Most used several methods, and continued to hurt themselves over months and years. The motivations given were varied, but included the wish to make themselves sexually unattractive or ill so that further assaults would be avoided. Some were trying to seek help, while others were punishing themselves for the abuse which they felt responsible for, or had enjoyed. De Young suggests that for some the act of injuring themselves can be seen as a form of ego reintegration, and quotes the case of a patient who would cut her arms after each sexual assault, which seemed to cleanse her of guilt and responsibility. This may be an example of the self-preservative type of violence.

The word 'trauma' is used here to cover both physical and sexual abuse. In my view there is a correlation between the extent of the trauma and the degree of powerlessness experienced by the child during the abusive acts. The child is often left with a feeling of being different and distant from others, and wary of future relationships. In some cases, this psychic closing off can be seen as a defence against the feelings aroused by the abuser. Passive resistance and dissociation of feeling seem to offer a type of defence against an overwhelming situation. One way to cope is to cut off from any feelings. Dissociation works because it gives a sense of personal control and power, in a situation where there is none. If left unresolved and not treated, it later carries over into relationships with others. It also carries over into the relationship within the self and becomes reinforced as a way of being.

The encaptive conflict can be compounded or triggered by later abuse because similar sorts of dynamics are involved. The 'relationship' or experience with the abuser can become internalised as an overwhelming, intrusive and dangerous figure in the psyche, yet one with whom there is deep involvement, and from whom it is hard to break free. The involvement can be especially complicated if the abuser is also someone who was previously non-abusive, trusted and loved. The abused consciously longs to have nothing more to do with the abuser, the whole experience, and to forget about it forever. Yet in sexual abuse the relationship is often explained to the child as a 'special' relationship. This creates an additional psychic dilemma when the child then simultaneously perceives and confuses the 'good' object with the 'bad' behaviour. The unbearable confusion leads to a splitting with the rage and horror internalised as part of the 'bad self', thus allowing the child to hold on to a fantasy of the originally loved and needed object as 'good'.

For example, a woman patient in her late thirties came into private psychotherapy with feelings of depression and hopelessness, feelings which quickly emerged in the therapy. In her twenties she had cut herself over a period of several years, and had long-term problems controlling the amount she ate. When I met her she was seriously overweight. About six months into the therapy she revealed that, while away at the weekend, she had realised that between the ages of 8 and 12 she had been regularly sexually abused by her uncle on frequent weekend visits. She had known about this, but understood and thought that it was part of her 'special' relationship with him that involved secrets. Once she realised she had been abused, the patient insisted she had no feelings on the subject, and for some time she did not speak again about her memories. Later she persuaded herself that if she had wanted to have stopped the abuse she could have done so, and that therefore she was responsible for it and wanted it to happen in the first place. She also felt guilty because she had betrayed the aunt who loved her. Both aunt and uncle had given her lots of presents and this contributed to the guilt she felt. If they were 'good', loving and generous then she became 'bad', hateful and ungrateful.

For people who have been sexually abused there is a desire to break free from this inner, abusive, malevolent figure – an internalised representation of the person who externally and physically threatened total possession and painful intrusion into the body. None the less, this desire to separate will stimulate an unconscious experience of rejection, abandonment and isolation. As explained at the beginning of this chapter this is linked to the earlier patterning, and the threat of loss leads in turn to low self-worth and feelings of despair. This conflict is unconscious, and one way of dealing with the uncomfortable sensations involved is to inflict pain on the body.

Furthermore, the body violation and actual penetration of the skin by cutting can also be seen as in part a repetition and unconscious re-enactment of the processes derived from the experience between abuser and abused. This time it takes place apparently under the young woman's own control and, at one level, because of her own wishes. By opening up the surface of the skin, aspects of the dynamics of the internalised experience are repetitiously evoked, though not necessarily consciously recollected. One function is seemingly to excise and expunge what was internalised, by getting it out of the body and externalising it by fixing it on the body surface. The angry violence is unconsciously directed both at the tyrannical, abusive object and the victim self. It is self-preservative and sado-masochistic – and ultimately self-destructive. In this sense what is appropriate anger at something which may have actually happened in childhood is both expressed and suppressed at the same time.

Anne, whom I discuss again in later chapters, had been sexually abused by an adult relative over a period of a few days when she was young. She had been terrified and physically hurt. In psychotherapy, Anne was able only occasionally to speak about the experience, and she felt very anxious about talking about it at all. She acknowledged no anger, and initially the very mention of the abuse provoked a period of cutting her arms and thighs. Four years after the abuse had happened, Anne began to try to control her body, initially by not eating, later by bingeing and vomiting, and laxative use, and then by cutting and attempting suicide. This seemed to provide a form of compensation for what she could not control, which were the thoughts and images that came into her mind about the abuse. What was difficult was expressing the images, sensations and feelings that haunted her in words, so that they too could begin to feel under control. The way in which the encaptive conflict emerged during the therapy is explored through detailed session material in Chapter 6.

Perhaps, for some of the young women, the attacks on the body were an attempt to recollect – to somehow bring to mind – earlier abusive experiences. The dissociation and inability to remember the abuse can, paradoxically, reflect a disordered inner preoccupation with it. This preoccupation can block internal space, preventing thoughts and feelings from being assimilated. This in turn would relate to the fact that no child could adequately integrate such a mind/body assault. The child is unable to integrate the abuse adequately at the level of its whole psychosomato-affective existence. The trauma may be grasped and interpreted by the child some time later than his or her original observation of it by 'after-revision' or 'deferred action' at a time when she is able to put it into words.

However, in the inner world of the child the trauma often remains 'thing-like' with little room for the use of fantasy and metaphorisation. It is then that the 'real' ritual and procedure of cutting, burning or hitting the body, or laying out the razor and counting out pills for an over-dose, comes to repeat the 'thing-like' quality that belonged to the earlier trauma. In my view the procedure becomes a reification of the internalised conflict. It is too difficult for the child to think or speak about what happened, and so it all remains in a 'concrete' and indigestible form. It is as raw and unprocessed as the action of wounding the skin and bleeding. In a similar way to the abuse which was 'something that happened', the cutting becomes 'something that I do'. The defence is an inhibition of thinking because the sensations and feelings involved in thought seem unbearable.

The physical, concrete nature of sexual abuse seems to leave little space or opportunity for any sense of sexual fantasy, but does leave the accompanying guilt often fuelled by a strict and punitive superego. If there was a body response of arousal or gratification, or a confused feeling of having been loved, the abused may be left with an idea about the 'betrayal of the body'. If the child knows, then or later, that something wrong took place, there is a sense of the body colluding with the aggressor, and of having been in conflict with the child's own mind. In this situation, the young woman uses harming herself as a way of punishing her body for any gratification she might have inadvertently experienced. The punishment can also be linked to a feeling that she, as a child, was somehow to blame. This belief often remains, despite other people's reassurances to the contrary. At a deep level, the child takes on the guilt and responsibility, and so feels the need to hurt herself and make reparation. The superego, formed from identification with, and processes linked to, feared authority figures, often seems to be especially cruel and critical among those who have been abused. There is also sometimes a perfectionist and strongly narcissistic element involved. In the following clinical extract, I want to draw attention to the power of the critical superego, and the weight and implications of carrying guilt for one patient.

Laura, who is discussed further in Chapter 6, disclosed sexual abuse by a relative. The authorities were involved but, for various circumstantial reasons, all charges were dropped, and Laura was left dealing with the after-effects of not just the abuse, but also the shock of the news for the immediate and extended family. One result of the disclosure of the abuse was that various family members no longer spoke to others, while Laura's immediate family tried to pretend that nothing had happened, and none of them spoke to her about it. Laura felt very guilty about everything that had occurred. It seemed to her that she was left carrying the guilt of the abuser, and a feeling of responsibility for the abuse, the disclosure and the rifts in the extended family.

The abuse had happened in the past on an intermittent basis over several years. Laura had never forgotten that it had happened, though she said that for a while she thought it had happened to this other girl who lived inside her, and not to herself. She spoke of her disgust about men and boys, but this left her feeling excluded among her college friends, who were all talking about who they wanted to go out with and who they fancied. She also felt disgusted by herself. Laura wanted no part in being female so she chose to wear men's clothes when she could – usually in large sizes and baggy so that her body shape could not be seen, and had her hair cut very short. Again, this set her apart from her friends.

I wondered whether at one level there was an embodying of the confusing figure who had abused her. This was a relative whom she had loved and trusted, but whom she now hated. Laura said she felt that she must have encouraged the abuse, that she felt guilty about this and that the responsibility lay in her body. She thought how she had looked had led to the abuse taking place. She spoke about how important it was now to cover up her body, and leave no room for anyone's imagination about the shapes underneath. Shortly after the disclosure she had begun to lose weight, but at the time of the therapy she was eating a great deal, so that her body form became less defined and she was able to build some sort of protective body armour. It almost seemed as if her 'guilty body' was being wrapped up and kept out of sight so that no further damage was done. Intellectually, Laura understood that the abuser was responsible and should feel guilty, but emotionally she took the blame. Her physical appearance and the deliberate self-harm represented the solutions she had found for this. She was reluctant to let go of them and think about the feelings involved.

The inner dynamics derived from childhood experiences of sexual or physical abuse – both being forms of mind/body assaults – involve mind and body memories, and mind and body fantasies linked to revenge, punishment or removal. The inner configurations derived from early object relations tend also to involve mind and body associations. The tensions arising from these compounded processes are relieved by attacking the body. Both sexual and physical abuse involve penetration of the body barrier, and as mentioned above, it is this that is unconsciously recollected by cutting. All violence and inappropriate touching of the body have their counterparts in the mind, and leave the traumatised young person fearful of further intrusions. Some of the same sensations may emerge as a result of witnessing physical attacks against siblings or another parent. Children who are witnesses to domestic violence are frequently fearful, angry and anxious, and can feel guilt and responsibility. One way of dealing with these feelings is 'letting rip' on the skin – a substitute for the direct articulation of anger which is often so difficult for young women to openly express.

Nicky, who often seemed to find herself in risky situations, was a friendly, open and overly trusting person. She seemed to insist on being cheery, and tried, as she said, always to look on the bright side. Following disclosure of sexual abuse by her mother's boyfriend, she had ended up having to move away to live with another member of her family. As she saw it, her mother had chosen her boyfriend over her daughter. Again, despite the involvement of the authorities and the abuser's previous convictions, the abuse was not proven, and he remained free to stay with Nicky's mother. One of the strangest aspects of the abuse was that, aware of the boyfriend's previous history, a social worker had regularly visited the home, and had involved Nicky and her brother in exercises encouraging them to say 'no' to inappropriate touching, and explaining how to protect themselves. It was only later that Nicky linked this to protection against sexual abuse from her mother's boyfriend, which ironically was actually happening at the same time.

In the therapy it seemed very hard for Nicky to think about how angry she was both with her mother and her mother's partner. Instead she wanted to cut herself, take drugs and get very drunk. She longed for a 'proper relationship', she wanted someone to love and to love her back, but she only met men who wanted sex, usually a one-night stand and nothing more. It was too difficult for her to connect with the rage she felt towards all the adults who had let her down, and to minimise the rage she inflicted on herself. Each new man whom she slept with would be, she hoped, the one to love her, and each betrayal left her feeling a little more desperate. In terms of the encaptive conflict, Nicky appeared enthralled by a non-protective, negligent abusive part of herself, revealed both in the sexual acting out and by the self-harm. Her cheeriness and positive wish to make everything better belied the deeply destructive aspects of her inner object relations. A constant preoccupation she voiced was about the part her mother had played, both while the abuse was taking place and after the disclosure. Did her mother care? Did her mother know? How could her mother have chosen him over Nicky? Nicky kept visiting her mother in an attempt to somehow find answers to her questions.

Key aspects that link abuse with self-harm are control and power. Both are owned by the perpetrator during the abuse, and retrieved and repeated by the abused when she harms herself. In this way there is an experienced traumatic interplay between the perpetrator and victim that is internalised and remembered through other relationships and behaviours. It builds on and consolidates the earlier patterns found in the encaptive conflict. It is this interplay between masochism and mastery that becomes 'intraplay', and it is this that is explored in the following section.

Aspects of masochism – the links with trauma and self-harm

Freud (1924) distinguished three forms of masochistic states of mind which he called erotogenic, feminine and moral. The erotogenic form of masochism, which is a form of sexual pleasure found in pain, was, he felt, ultimately the basis for the other two categories of masochism. This state of mind underlay many types of sexual relationship, and linked back to infantile sexuality. In his description of feminine masochism, Freud saw it as a possibility for either sex placed 'in a characteristically female situation' of passivity, or being hurt or injured (1924: 162). There was a point reached where pain, or unpleasure, reached a state of such tension that some sort of internal excitation of the sexual instinct occurred. The experience would result in a form of body memory, which would act as some sort of base for future similar experiences.

The link between masochism and its counterpart, sadism, can be understood by seeing masochism as a derivative of the death and destructive instinct as described in Chapter 2. The libido diverts the instinct outwards into the external world, where it can be described as 'the destructive instinct, the instinct for mastery, or the will to power' (Freud 1924: 163). The part that is transposed outside on to others is sadism, while the portion that remains inside the person directed against the self is masochism. This interrelationship between sadism and masochism can change at any point, so that what is projected outside can be re-introjected, and so on. It is also part of any normal infantile and childhood development. Moral masochism is not so clearly linked to sexual excitement, although the erotic component is still present. On one level it seems that it is the suffering itself which is important. Freud linked this to a sense of guilt which was mostly unconscious, and to the need for punishment which the actual experience of suffering fulfils. The person then experiences some pleasure at their own destruction and suffering.

When childhood sexual abuse takes place, the child has been prematurely sexualised, forced to grow sexually but unable to grow emotionally. As mentioned above, the memory of the body pain from both physical and sexual abuse leads to some sort of body/mind correlation around pain, and an inner tension contributing to excitation. This is either deeply repressed or dissociated, remaining in some split-off corner of the mind. However, mental representations are greatly affected and chaotically influence the internal world. There can be an unconscious compulsion to repeat the experience, and masochistic, destructive attacks on the body partly fulfil that function.

The sense of guilt linked to masochism can be conscious, partly conscious or repressed. Children usually feel that things are their fault, so it is not unexpected that there is a strong sense of guilt around the idea that something wrong has taken place. Furthermore, in the case of sexual abuse, the 'something wrong' that has happened is usually a secret, and most children who have been abused believe that, as they took part in it, it must be their fault. The child can end up carrying the guilt of the adult abuser, as in the example of Laura. Another aspect of guilt is a feeling that somehow as a child they could have prevented what happened. In sexual abuse, the abusive relationship is often hidden, seen as a 'special' secret and yet stigmatised, and this aspect is also recalled and re-enacted by the secrecy and feelings of stigma associated with cutting and scarring the body. By internalising the dynamic processes, the child may keep the abuser safe as an external 'good object', and this may explain the link between masochism and separation difficulties. This is strongest when the parents have been the source of the trauma. It is as if the young person keeps close to the abusing parent as part of their own masochistic actions. This point is picked up by Glenn (1984), who comments that the child (who has been hurt by the parents) seeks pain-producing objects in order to imagine his parents' presence.

Aspects of mastery – the links with abuse and self-harm

The concept of mastery inevitably involves a relationship with another – initially externally, then as an internalised object. Mastery reflects a desire to ignore or neutralise the other person's wishes or needs. There is no space for difference or otherness – again, interestingly, no separation. The other person/victim is seen and treated as a part-object available to be used. This is why mastery is so destructive. Dorey writes: 'the aim is to reduce the other to the function and status of a totally assailable object' (1986: 323). This is achieved first through perversion, when mastery takes place through seduction of a sexual partner; second through an obsessional configuration demonstrated in the field of power and duty through force. When a child is abused, the abuser may use both configurations of mastery to get his way. The abuser often wants to believe that the abused is subject and dependent, and agrees to what is happening. In some situations the person seeking mastery makes an actual imprint on the body of the other to confirm their power and control. In adult sado-masochistic relationships this can be made through the use of a whip or bondage equipment.

When this relationship of mastery is internalised, and for some of the young women repeated by deliberate self-harm, there is then a corresponding need to mark and wound. The sado-masochistic elements are imprinted and reflected in the slashes on the arms and legs. These can be seen to replicate the marks of enslavement and imprisonment to the wishes of another, previously experienced at an emotional level when the actual abuse took place, but then internalised. At an even deeper level they represent the dynamics of the encaptive conflict based on the earlier inner object relations. The cuts may be seen as symbols of this and of what has subsequently happened to the self – scarred through emotional abuse, physical abuse or internally 'marked' by sexual abuse.

When mastery takes an obsessive form, the central issues become those of domination and appropriation. The obsessive is compelled by internal destructive drives which are perverse and narcissistic, and are then projected out into the external world. The body is treated in a perverse way. Perversion is used here in the analytic sense, in which 'the individual afflicted does not feel free to obtain sexual genital satisfaction, but instead feels subjected to a compulsive activity that takes over and involves unconscious hostility' (Welldon 1988: 155). The recipient of such an obsessive form of mastery submits and internalises the experience, and, later, compulsively repeats the experience – this time having power and control over the destruction. Welldon reminds us that victims of perverse actions or attitudes will not necessarily act in a perverse way themselves, but there is great strain and difficulty in achieving mental equilibrium if there has been an experience of perverse parental behaviour in early life (1988: 156).

At times, these aspects of mastery fuse into one another, and these unconscious formations contribute to the need of victims to cut themselves. For some patients, cutting takes an obsessive form. These abusive experiences probably exacerbate already over-stimulated internal destructive and aggressive drives.

There is a further aspect of mastery to consider, what Freud termed 'the instinct for mastery'. This can be a transformative activity, a way of changing the death instinct, and therefore controlling destructive urges (1924). Another description is of the instinct for mastery as the driving force behind children's play, as 'the impulse to make over in the mind some overpowering experience so as to make oneself master of it' (Freud 1920: 16).

The need to repeat an abusive experience through attacking the body

Repeating an experience is often linked to the need to remember what happened. Repeating and remembering are closely interwoven. The repetition of hostility, in the form of the act of harming the body and the feelings associated with that act, is a kind of remembering, albeit an unconscious one. In turn, remembering as a conscious mental act involves some form of repetition. Uncovering the unconscious need to compulsively repeat earlier experiences is the cornerstone of analytic understanding and treatment. If we repress something and try not to think about it, it will seek to return even more powerfully through dreams, fantasies, symptoms and acting out. With increasing awareness, the repressed or denied comes into consciousness, and so can be understood. However, repeatedly attacking the body can be seen as a form of mastery by working through, or can be seen as related to the most instinctual part of our unconscious and a form of sado-masochism. In other words, the need for repetition can either be seen as a process that allows us slowly to gain control of a situation that was previously out of our control – a form of revenge and so triumph over childhood trauma; or it can be seen as a process through which we endlessly punish ourselves, and perversely and narcissistically gratify that urge for punishment. One is a process of mastery, the other of masochism. What I am suggesting here is that there may be a fusion or interrelationship between the two inner processes in those who are cutting.

One effect of repeated cutting is that this re-creates, represents and may reinforce already embedded and burned-in body memories. Traumatic repetition is, like many physical over-reactions, an excessive response. When this happens the repetition, rather than leading to the process of transformation via mastery, becomes a more self-defeating and masochistic process. This is linked to the belief that 'this is what I am' (guilty, hateful, angry, trapped and so on) – 'so this is what I do' (cut, hurt, bleed, feel sore). Both the transformative and self-defeating aspects of mastery are blended in a given action. The danger, as previously discussed, is that the behaviour contains its own addictive aspects. The term 'traumataphilia' is used to describe this unconscious and compulsive need to repeat abusive experiences. One possibility for interrupting this compulsion is that through the therapeutic relationship some freedom from this need can be found.

Fusion and intraplay in the after-effects of trauma which lead to self-harm

The intrapsychic dynamics become fused with one another quite quickly. In other words, any distinction between the self and the other object involved in the traumatic experience become blurred and indistinct. The person who is harming herself demonstrates aspects of omnipotent self-sufficiency, and becomes identified with the aggressor. In contrast, another form of fusion that can emerge is with the victim – corresponding to the opposite of identification with the aggressor. This is where the person is unable to project, or to maintain the projection of aggressive feelings, away from the self. In other words, the person cannot turn passive into active aggression.

> The idealised object, still largely fused with the primary narcissistic self, is seen not as omnipotent, but as a victim; while the subject, instead of turning passivity into activity and externalising the aggression or imitating the aggressor, turns the aggression against himself, becoming one with the victim-object.
>
> (Orgel 1974: 531)

The roots of this state of mind belong in infancy to a type of primitive identification with a parent who is unable to provide a safe focus for the projection of aggressive instinctual impulses, and the satisfaction of the infant's needs. The developing infant requires someone who can respond to the discharge of aggression by an appropriate balance of loving counter-aggression, and direction-giving limit setting. When this happens there is a limit set on self-injury, such as biting and scratching, which can establish a prototype for later experiences. If this does not happen then aggressive impulses can become over-stimulated, and feel dangerously out of control.

Infants who are depressed because of failures in attachment can slowly become self-destructive, as there is no one on whom they can reliably vent their aggression in the outer world. The only available object is the young child's own body, as she is incapable of expressing any aggression in an object relationship. This is not the same as the sado-masochistic relationships discussed above; rather the experience is of an inability to defend against the aggression. Indeed the victim role is sought out, and there is an immediate identification as potential victim. For young women who have experienced emotional neglect, or some form of abuse, there is little sense of safety and appropriate limit setting. They experience alongside the trauma a form of regression to a place where no boundaries are maintained, and there is no safe place for angry and frightened feelings to be contained and managed.

In the following clinical material the patient demonstrated this fusion and intraplay of aggressor and victim. At times it seemed that her obsessive compulsion to repeat through self-harm was mainly fuelled by perverse and narcissistic drives, and there was little sense of her gaining control through her actions, or making any change to the way she coped. Martha was a woman in her early forties who was brought to private supervision by a colleague. She had received psychiatric treatment in the past, and had had previous counselling. She was referred by her doctor for counselling at the surgery, and then taken on for open-ended work. However, nothing seemed to curtail her cutting, which she had been doing since adolescence. She cut whenever she felt upset by others. This occurred frequently, since she seemed easily overwhelmed by circum-stances and her own sense of hopelessness. She had also taken several overdoses in the past, and this threat remained. During her therapy she spoke of her inability to see herself as ever being different. She was married but lived with her husband as 'brother and sister', finding the idea of sexual contact repugnant. Martha was not able to work, but sometimes carried out clothes alterations for neighbours in return for a small fee.

During therapy it became apparent that this woman's fantasies were linked to a neglectful and indifferent mother, later compounded by inappropriate sexual touching by her grandfather. She felt unsafe away from home, and found the short journey to the sessions highly stressful. She was emotionally very fragile, and so the cutting seemed to provide a boundary for her, and some form of identification. If she cut she knew who she was – 'hopeless Martha' she called herself. Her expectations were that she would be let down, or left, or forgotten about, and this inevitably put the therapist under enormous pressure. Martha's belief that cutting was the necessary and only possible solution revealed her omnipotence and narcissism. She could do it alone, it worked, and cost much less than the counselling. She was frightened at any display of her feelings, and seemed to be 'at home' with her victim status. Her envy and rage were muted, but very powerfully projected on to the counsellor who felt buffeted by different emotions. These ranged from an anxious, gnawing concern about Martha's welfare, to impotent frustration and fury – a state no doubt experienced by Martha's husband in their sexless marriage.

It seemed that Martha's inner world was primarily populated by two fused figures structuring the encaptive conflict: one a poor, deprived victim who needed to bribe, wheedle and manipulate to get anything for herself; the other a denying, all-powerful, cruel figure who could do anything and needed no one. The struggle in the counselling was to see if there was a part of Martha that could allow these aspects to be recognised. Over several years it became clearer that for Martha thinking about these sensations was too dangerous. She continued to cut, especially after sessions where her self-made equilibrium was threatened, and indeed she spoke again about death as the only real answer to her 'hopeless state'. The destructive part of Martha seemed to gain strength as it came under increased threat, and the splits were firmly maintained. It seemed as if it were not possible for Martha to have a sense of unity of her self, and to bear the pain of insight. The counsellor felt increasingly close to being submerged, and in the supervision we discussed possible ways that this could be held and managed. The ending was precipitated by the counsellor feeling that she needed to strengthen the liaison with Martha's doctor, a move with which Martha did not agree. She felt that the counsellor had betrayed and let her down by this idea, and said that she would not continue the treatment.

This case suggests that Martha's conflicts, derived from the maternal environment and later abuse, might well have been traceable back over at least three generations. One could speculate that Martha's mother was repeating her own experiences of parental handling, and that she too might have been abused by her father – the grandfather who abused Martha.

'Cutting off one's nose to spite one's face'

The unconscious encaptive conflict is fuelled by, and interacts with, instinctual aggressive processes. Instinctual processes are also affected and linked experientially to the maternal environment and early parental handling. The internal and external aspects are mutually influential and adaptive. This dialectical process is graphically illustrated by Ritvo (1984), who outlines the developmental sequence observed in the behaviour of a 21-month-old boy. Initially as a baby boy he bites at his mother's breast as a way of gaining pleasure, yet by a year old this has evolved into an organised aggressive response, usually as a result of frustration. At this stage it is still directed outwards – as he is biting, hitting or throwing actual objects. After an incident when the infant throws a glass, another child is injured and the 1-year-old boy is told off. In the months following this event, whenever the small boy is discomfited, alarmed or spoken to sharply, he says he is being bitten – for example, he complains that the nappy rubbing him is biting. Ritvo's suggestion is that the mother's anger, worry and sharp words when the boy threw the glass may have been a dynamic factor in the timing of the boy's reversal of the drive, turning it against his own body.

The observation showed that by 21 months, the external object had become the little boy's own body. In other words the internal feelings were being dealt with through the use of his own body. This action was reinforced by the boy's fear of losing the love of the adult if his aggression were to be directed outwards. This example demonstrates the process involved in the developing use of the body to express psychic conflict – the child uses the image and perception of the body to externalise and master his aggression. The instinctual processes are affected and altered according to the experience of object relations. The resulting process turns back on the child in the form of fear. In adolescence there is a re-emergence of the strength and danger of instinctual processes such as aggression, and a re-emergence of ways of managing it – although these are obviously adapted to more age-appropriate modes of expression. The emerging aggression can become inhibited or uninhibited – either way it can feel uncontrollable.

Inhibited aggression

The development of these internal processes is also affected by other external aspects including social and cultural factors. It is well known that the socialisation of girls, despite the widespread knowledge of assertiveness training and the need to voice feelings, still carries a deeply embedded prohibition against aggressive behaviours and outward expressions of anger. The threat of such behaviours is the loss of sexual identity and attractiveness, alongside the loss of a favoured female characteristic of loving concern and service. The result is that young women's anger towards both men and other women can be redirected against the self or the body, or against the even more powerless such as their children. An accompanying aspect is the tendency for women to seek approval from other people, which leads to compliant behaviour.

Alongside these social aspects there are more subtle processes which lead to the inhibition of aggression. One is repression, which serves as an obstruction between the different layers of the conscious and the unconscious. While this can be seen as a horizontal obstruction, another process – dissociation – can be seen as a vertical barrier, separating and isolating the traumatic experience, so that the central self escapes from the pain and the reality of what has happened. It is not just an overloading of the circuits; there is a breakdown between the event and any sense of its meaning. With both forms of inhibition, all the complicated conflicts between opposing emotions, such as love and hate, are kept out of conscious awareness. There can also be an inhibition of anger because of fear of what the effect on another person might be. A further complication is that when angry feelings cannot be directed outwards, either verbally or physically, it can be because there is a sense of the inadequacy or fragility of the other person. For example, some of the patients seen for psychotherapy would talk about needing to protect their parents, especially their mothers who might not be able to cope or manage. The secret cutting thus helped the young women by relieving the tension of such inhibited feelings, and at the same time in their minds no one was being hurt by the action. The fear of damaging another person can be dealt with through psychotherapy.

Uncontrolled aggression

Sometimes sensations of aggression can feel uncontrollable – this is especially true during adolescence. This could be compounded by an inability to mentally represent feelings of anger and fury – in other words, to put such affects into words. Fonagy's understanding of what he calls the capacity to 'mentalise' defines this as 'the capacity to conceive of conscious and unconscious mental states in oneself and others' (1991: 641). He points out that the ability to represent the idea of an affect or sensation is crucial in the achievement of control over overwhelming affect. He goes on to argue that the development of this capacity is dependent on a degree of consistency and safety in early object relationships, and what he calls 'good enough' psychic functioning in the parents to 'empower the process of internalisation' (1991: 642).

The inability or inadequacy to mentally represent affects then compounds the sense that they are uncontrollable. The experience of this functional disturbance leads to action. This takes the form of turning the anger inwards against the self (predominantly found in young women; cutting is one example of this), or, paradoxically, a complete lack of control of aggression in the external world (predominantly found in young men), or an experience where both happen – extreme aggression inflicted both on self and other.

Pithers (1983) describes his work with a group of young people who violently acted out feelings either towards themselves or each other. Conventional psychotherapy was inappropriate, so Pithers used an activity-based approach. He writes: 'if I tried to remove "fuck" or "shit" from their vocabulary little else would remain and the unsafe little structure would collapse, their social behaviour is inelegant, their controls primitive' (1983: 2).

One of the young people whom Pithers describes is Kim, a tall and powerful skinhead noted for her quick temper and instant violent retaliation. His compelling account continues that on one evening she knocked out one of the boys in the group with little effort, because he referred to her as female. Kim tried to disguise her gender because she hated being female. The denial included trying to get rid of her breasts, which were large and prominent. Kim had tried to remove them a number of times, including by using a hacksaw. Her left breast was the most mutilated, and was subject to a recurring infection for which she was given a large dressing, which only served to accentuate what she wanted to get rid of. Pithers gives a moving account of containing her threatening violence towards him, by getting her to rock him in an activity which he used to great effect with deprived young people, though usually the other way round, in that he would rock them. In this instance:

> eventually she began to hold me more firmly and, as sometimes happens the experiences overwhelmed me. I began to cry and as I did she held me more tightly. Until as she struggled to contain it she held my head to her breasts.
>
> (Pithers 1983: 11)

Pithers believed that this was a key moment in Kim's experience, and one that they could both talk about in terms of Kim starting to accept that she was female. If aggressive processes and sexual activity are key elements in adolescence, they can become especially important in inarticulate young people with only rudimentary controls. Adolescents like this have few controls for dealing with overwhelming feelings; their response is based on impulsive action and accompanied by an impoverished inner world. When the perception of the world is crude and simple, the conditions for developing reflective and thoughtful behaviour do not exist. Then the response is based on impulse and acting out. To change this, and develop the ability to think about one's own feelings and other people's, there needs to be modelling or encouragement by a respected adult to help the child or adolescent to think imaginatively. Through such a process there develop possibilities for containing, transferring, redirecting and in other ways utilising aggression in personally satisfying and socially significant directions.

Self-punishment

When the young women spoke about hating and punishing themselves, they demonstrated the relentless pressure from the demands of their superego. There often appeared to be no respite from this internal critical judge. In self-punishment the patient is treating her body as an object worthy of chastisement. The self-punishment is not just taking the place of disciplining someone else, nor just where the self has become merged with the external object, but it is also because of the strength of hateful feelings themselves. The aggressive element can be both active or passive. In the above example Kim was actively punishing herself for being born female, which she felt to be a passive condition.

The self-punishment can be linked to fantasies about the developing sexual body, masturbation or sexual fantasies, and, as discussed in the context of sexual abuse, can be linked to sexual feelings and feelings of guilt and shame. The aggressive and sexual aspects can be conflated. For example, a highly disturbed young man was seen in a team assessment at the clinic. He was aggressive towards others and himself. The disguised sexual element in his aggression was revealed as he was leaving. When thanked by the psychiatrist for 'coming' (to the appointment), the boy became agitated, commenting that he had never heard anything so disgusting in his life.

Self-punishment can reflect a sexualisation of aggression, and there is a clear sexual aspect to penetration and opening up of the skin, whether by razor, knife, cigarette or through piercing. Bovensiepen (1995) puts this perspective plainly when he suggests that as girls attack themselves with sharp objects, such as a razor, there is a concomitant fantasy about the violent penis (bad object) penetrating into the containing object. This sort of fantasy can be seen to link back to the fears of patients who had been sexually abused, and were using the attacks on their bodies as a way of controlling the awful thoughts and feelings about their experiences. As mentioned above, the very action of cutting the skin paradoxically recalls the physical experience of the body violation during the abuse – this time self-perpetrated. The dilemma is how to manage and contain the violent aggression, so that it can be redirected in a constructive, though not necessarily conformist manner. The focus then is to help the patient believe in the possibility of benign relationships both intrapsychically and interpsychically.

The redirection of aggressive processes towards the self can also be seen as serving to restore some threatened relationship through repentant self-punishment. The act can be seen as representing retaliatory abandonment directed against objects whose loss is feared. In other words, an angry defiance – 'If you leave me then I'll leave you too'. The aggressive action against the self may be the conflict between needs, and the anticipation of the apparent frustration of these needs.

For example, a supervisee described her work with a woman in her twenties who had a history of cutting and overdosing. The therapy was primarily of a supportive nature which this woman found a great help. She had become increasingly dependent, and found the holiday breaks very difficult. These feelings of being let down and abandoned by the therapist became overwhelming before the summer break, when the woman spoke about her wish to finally end her life. She confided in the therapist that she had managed to get a prescription of powerful pain-killers from the doctor, which she might use while the therapist was away. Naturally the therapist was very concerned, and brought this anxiety to supervision. In the supervision we discussed the ways in which the therapist might both interpret the actions, and convey a sense to the client of 'being held' in the mind of the therapist over the break. We also examined the therapist's feelings of resentment about being manipulated into this anxious position, and how she might resolve that within herself. After the break I heard that the therapist had discussed her concern with her patient, commenting on the patient's warm feelings towards the sweet and concerned doctor in comparison to her perception of the therapist as uncaring. There had been talk over whether the pills should stay in the consulting room over the break, but the patient had said she would keep but not use them – they remained a security – and the patient survived the holiday.

Several of the patients described in this chapter were women long past adolescence. In the next chapter the link between self-harm and an adolescent state of mind is explored.

Chapter 4

Predisposing factors in adolescence linked to self-harm

This chapter explores the particular predisposing factors of body and self-development that occur during adolescence, and that are linked to self-harm. Before going any further it might be worthwhile to emphasise a central schema used throughout this book, namely that attacking the body is a symbolic satisfaction of different internal and conflictual states of mind. In this chapter, the conflicts particularly explored are those linked to sexuality and separation–individuation. These are the conflicts particularly associated with leaving home and growing up, and the various troublesome oscillations involved during this time of transition. In that sense it may be suggested that some of the psychic dilemmas so characteristic of adolescence are the same oscillations that characterise the deeply embedded encaptive conflict – those involved in wanting and leaving, possession and rejection. Self-harm typically begins in adolescence, and is characterised by an adolescent state of mind, even when the person harming themselves may be long past adolescence. An adolescent mind-set is not necessarily chronologically based, but can remain powerfully present and unresolved and so reactivated under pressure.

There is an extensive and well-known literature on adolescence and the phases of adolescence, written from a variety of analytic perspectives (e.g. Blos 1962; Copley 1993; Frankel 1998; Laufer 1995; Laufer and Laufer 1984, 1989). All these analytic writers agree on the inevitable immaturity of the adolescent, and the intense feelings and sense of confused identity and unpredictability powerfully present during this time of transition. Anderson reminds us of the increasing use of projective identification in adolescence, and that the target for many of the projections is the parents themselves (2000: 12). Earlier experiences from infancy and childhood – for example, anxiety associated with the Oedipal conflict – tend to be reawakened. With this the possibility emerges of resolving, or at least reordering, old experiences. This is helped by the general characteristic of adolescence that it is a time of great energy and intellectual development, with accompanying curiosity about physical, sexual and emotional changes in oneself and others. The perilous journey to become an independent and sexual adult involves tracing a path through the impact of puberty, finding a sexual identity, leaving parents and home, and coping with all the associated and ambivalent feelings of being left. This journey is usually problematic for the majority of adolescents, but I concentrate on some of the experiences that are specific to adolescent girls which may throw some light on the question of self-harm.

There are two clear developmental tasks of adolescence – the first to do with puberty and the negotiation of sexual development; the second with the separation from the parents and the development of individuality. Obviously these tasks have their emotional roots in early infancy and are present throughout childhood in an overt or covert manner. They can also remain emotionally unresolved for many people well on into adult life, and so, to emphasise once again, have meaning beyond chronology.

Characteristics of the adolescent mind-set and the link to self-harm

There are five states of mind that are familiar in adolescence and are also characteristic of self-harming behaviour. The first is the intensification of aggressive impulses and processes, which, as already mentioned, is also clearly an aspect of cutting. Growing up is essentially an aggressive act. Winnicott put it succinctly: 'If in the fantasy of early growth, there is contained *death*, then in adolescence there is contained *murder* . . . because growing up means taking the parents' place' (1971: 169). Such murderous feelings can be acted out or turned inwards, as was discussed in Chapter 3, and as stated previously, aggressive processes fuel the encaptive conflict in those who self-harm. For Winnicott, the only cure for adolescence, a time he describes as the 'doldrums', is the passing of time.

A second state of mind particularly familiar during adolescence is narcissism, which precedes the consolidation of finding alternative love objects. This is shown through grandiose self-sufficiency, omnipotence and auto-erotic activities. I suggest that all of these characterise self-harming, where there is a belief that the solution found is the only one, inflicted alone, and with an aspect of auto-eroticism and masturbation involved. In adolescents generally, the result of such narcissism is an overvaluation of the self and self-centredness, alongside touchiness and bad temper. Such narcissism can be linked to difficulties in giving up the gratifying parent, and also to the dilemma of breaking free from a tyrannical inner object relationship.

A third state of mind is hypersensitivity and heightened feeling, with fantasy expectations and anxieties about others. This seems to have a link with the quality of the events recounted as the trigger to an incident of cutting. There often appeared to be a watchfulness in those who self-harmed about the responses of other people, and what they might be saying or thinking. When reported, this can sometimes appear to the therapist as just a random remark or casual encounter. For some of the young women seen for psychotherapy, people's actions or responses often felt too much or were the last straw – and so the cutting relieved the immediate pressure caused by the trigger experience. In psychotherapy, as is discussed in some of the clinical extracts, some of the patients were vigilant about my responses – including any perceived gestures – demonstrating their anxieties both about rejection and being taken over.

The fourth state of mind is the tendency of the adolescent to turn to action. This can be a defence against painful feelings, or parental dependence, but also a form of mastery and means of self-expression. It naturally links to all the physical changes and the increase in energy. Cutting is obviously an action that takes precedence over thinking and reflecting.

The fifth and last adolescent state of mind that links to the propensity to attack the body is the preoccupation with death. In adolescence the acceptance of mortality occurs alongside the capacity to procreate and give birth, and both independence and uncertainty result from such juxtaposition. There is both reassurance and excitement in the knowledge that mortality can be manipulated. Although cutting is not about death or killing the body, there is an aspect of the destruction that is linked to the preoccupation with death and the death instinct, as was discussed in Chapter 2.

All these adolescent states of mind can be transitory, positive and part of the maturing process. When they become stuck, destructive and defeating they can lead to action directed either outwards as in delinquency, or inwards as in self-harm. The direction taken is often closely linked to gender. As a generalisation, adolescent girls tend to direct inwards and towards their physical bodies. For example, in a customary way the girl's narcissism is frequently displayed through excessive preoccupation with how she looks, or the state of her nails, face and hair. This self-absorption paradoxically contributes to a feeling of alienation from the body. The body is experienced as something 'other', something that is done to, altered and modified, and it seems that this intimacy alongside the detachment leads to the possibility of attacking the body. In a similar way hypersensitivity is commonly experienced about body image and perception. Impulsive acting out on the body reduces the tension from conflictual internal states, and the control and ownership displayed by deliberate self-injury alleviates uncertainty. Paradoxically, with some forms of acting out on the body, young women may experience power and autonomy at the same time as sometimes becoming physically weaker and more dependent on others. This is especially the case following an overdose or with an eating disorder.

Body changes and the need for control

The whole experience of uncontrollable body changes during puberty contributes to the feelings of excitement, confusion and fear that are inevitably part of early adolescence. Both boys and girls experience profound body changes as part of the development of their capacity to produce children, and these physical changes powerfully affect the way young people feel, think and fantasise about themselves, and also what they imagine others are thinking about them. For girls the changes usually take place earlier and more dramatically than for boys, as there is an alteration in the shape of the body with the development of breasts and more rounded hips and thighs. Such changes inevitably happen and are out of the girl's control – they can be welcomed or not, but their physical presence signals an end to childhood. As the changes take place the self and body can feel disconnected from each other, with the self as a fragile container almost at the mercy of uncontrollable physical sensations and urges.

The effect of such uncontrollable changes and the associated fantasies can contribute to a feeling of bodily estrangement – the sense of the body as different, and as being an object, something apart and separate from the self. This then is a crucial feature involved in the practice of harming through cutting – the body becomes something that can be 'dealt with' or 'punished and disciplined', and so is indirectly controlled and dealt with through specific physical attacks. For the person who harms themselves the body is being treated as something other and apart from the self. In this way it provides both the target and receptacle for unmanageable feelings and uncontrollable instinctual impulses. This new relationship to the body is fundamentally one of disconnection, not integration, although the paradox is that only through disconnection can the body become the containing object for the fragile and fragmenting self.

The use of the female body for attack and punishment is of course a well-established cultural perspective – many men have treated women in this way for centuries. In some ways the female body can be seen as something that is hurt, hit and penetrated. Inevitably this cultural acceptance of oppression, physical attack and detachment from the actual person is internalised and can re-emerge as part of the girl's confusion and fantasy about her own developing body during adolescence. It is also present in much popular culture where women are hit, slashed, raped, murdered and skinned.

The idea of the female body as an object 'appropriate' for violent attack is illustrated by Bret Easton Ellis' character in *American Psycho* who tortures and maims his victims.

> I keep shooting nails into her hands until they're both covered – nails bunched together, twisted over each other in places, making it impossible for her to try and sit up. . . . The fingers I haven't nailed I try to bite off, almost succeeding on her left thumb which I manage to chew all the flesh off of, leaving the bone exposed . . . I occasionally stab at her breasts, accidentally (not really) slicing off one of her nipples through the bra.
>
> (Easton Ellis 1991: 245–6)

The novel *The Silence of the Lambs*, also a highly successful film, describes a series of gruesome murders which involve 'skinning' the female victims. We eventually find out the horrible reason why. In this extract Starling, a police agent, is reporting on the latest finding.

> The system requires brief concise statements. Starling had to come up with some.
>
> 'White female, late teens or early twenties, shot to death, lower torso and thighs flayed – .'
>
> 'Starling, the Index already knows he kills young white women and skins their torsos – What's new here Starling?'
>
> 'This is the sixth victim, the first one scalped, the first one with triangular patches taken from the back of the shoulders, the first one shot in the chest, the first one with a cocoon in her throat' 'You forgot broken fingernails'
>
> 'No sir, she's the second one with broken finger nails'
>
> (Harris 1999: 89)

In contemporary society a great deal of apparent change has taken place, opening up the potential opportunities for adolescent girls to successfully achieve the transition into adulthood. People are more aware of violence against women, rights of women and sexism. Much is written about women's sense of themselves, their bodies, their sexuality and good relationships, and all this is accessible to adolescent girls through popular culture as well as education. However, it seems that for many of those who repeatedly harm themselves, their body is still seen as a suitable target for destructive attack and injury. The body remains the symbolic location for, and enemy of, the upheaval that is happening in their mind. The young women's experience of themselves and who they are appears vulnerable and not robust enough to withstand the confused emotions and sensations.

Frankel (1998), commenting on the themes of disintegration and fragmentation that link to this sense of fragility, notes that it is present in all adolescents, both boys and girls, but to varying degrees. He describes all the bodily changes that bring forth such feelings of disintegration and fragility: voice breaking and the emergence of facial hair in boys; the bouts of acne in both sexes which can lead to great self-consciousness; and growth spurts in both sexes which can lead to feelings of disorientation. Without doubt one of the major changes for girls is the onset of menstruation, which in contemporary Western societies is often experienced with a mixture of dismay and excitement. As with other body changes, beginning her periods can have an undermining effect on the adolescent's sense of control over her body, and some girls experience strong feelings of shame and disgust.

Several analytic studies emphasise a link between menstruation and cutting parts of the body. For example, a study by Rosenthal *et al.* (1972) highlights the two central aspects as lack of control over what is happening in the body, and the shame about menstruation. Many of the patients in their study referred for harming themselves perceived the start of their periods as something to fear and feel miserable about; they also often had irregular periods, which would exacerbate the feeling that their body was out of control. This finding seems to confirm the link made between attacking the body and the conception of the body as something apart from the self. There is an intriguing link between the idea of uncontrolled bleeding and controlled bleeding. Some theorists have looked at the symbolic connection of blood between menstruation and cutting, and suggested cutting as a form of vicarious menstruation, and a displacement from the genitals (e.g. Deutsch 1944). Bettelheim (1955) saw the 'wound' to the body as symbolising the vagina and menstruation, but thought it was an attempt to identify with the mother and help the transition from childhood to adulthood – such a positive attempt to identify with mother is not confirmed in my experience, although the identification could be connected to the anxiety about rejection by or separation from an all-powerful mother.

Sexual development and identity

It is well accepted that the development towards adult sexuality tends to be difficult and disrupted. Any infantile sexual interest in the parents may briefly re-emerge, but is usually redirected towards other adolescents and outside the family. The obvious way to achieve active adult sexual identity is through relationship and physical involvement with another person, but most adolescents begin to explore something about their developing sexual desires through masturbation. It is generally acknowledged that girls, in comparison to their male counterparts, masturbate less frequently and more indirectly, and rarely have spontaneous orgasms through masturbation. For boys the discovery of masturbation leads to the development of a sense of autonomy, and can be used as a way of soothing and comforting themselves.

Laufer notes that the difference between attitudes to female and male masturbation may be defined as 'a difference in attitude to the use of the hand for masturbatory activity' (1982: 301). The unconscious meaning of the hand as identifying with the mother's active earlier handling of the child's body leads to an experience for the adolescent girl of identification of her body with that of the hated mother's body. Laufer links self-cutting to the female patient's fear of giving in to the regressive wish to be passively cared for: 'the self-damage was preceded by an outburst of uncontrolled hostility against the mother, the sexual partner or the analyst' (1982: 298).

These insights might lead us to enquire what other forms masturbation might take in young women. As noted earlier in the book, aspects of the repetitive harming of the skin can be seen to provide in part a masturbatory activity for some adolescent girls. This is partly because of the feelings of self-soothing that are evoked and which co-exist alongside the libidinal gratification produced through the activity. Daldin takes up this idea of sexual satisfaction, and pushes it to the point where he emphasises the pleasurable component of cutting the skin, and suggests that the sensation can be seen as 'an orgasm equivalent' (1990: 281). His reasoning is that the adolescent who harms herself is neither able to contain her sexual and aggressive thoughts and urges through masturbation and masturbation fantasies, nor indeed to take control of them other than by enactment through harming herself. While thought provoking, his rather masculine, drive-oriented interpretation with its emphasis on sexual satisfaction denies the more sensual, sensation-based experience of female sexuality. The self-soothing and comfort-seeking nature of the practice of cutting appears to connect more, albeit in a perverse way, with the experience of the maternal erotic. Indeed it becomes in some situations a strange sort of perverse mothering and a painful form of self-care.

Other aspects of sexuality and control include the site/sight of the genitals. Although at times a boy may be embarrassed by uncontrolled aspects of his penis, he can learn about it and have more control over it and his physical self, because he has direct visual and physical access. Bernstein (1990) explores the genital anxieties that girls experience. One problem lies in the girl's inability to mentally represent her genitals – she does not have ready visual or complete tactile access, although a boyfriend or doctor might have. When she does touch her genitals, there is a spread of sensation to another area, so the experience is diffused rather than focused as it is for a boy. A central anxiety is around the issue of penetration, and the sense that the vagina is a passive and inert body opening over which there is no control. Linked to this lack of control are anxieties over body fluids – wetness and menstruation – which may link back to worries over toilet training. Cross (1993) in her illuminating exploration of these issues suggests that because of the girl's lack of knowledge about the inside of her body, the boundary between penis and vagina may be rather vague, and the penis may be experienced as the 'other within'. This anticipates the later 'other within' – the foetus – and affects a girl's mental representation of her body. This experience may lead to all sorts of feelings about sexual involvement, including avoidance of sex. Such avoidance is a way of gaining both physical and psychological ownership of the body, and is in contrast with the majority of adolescent boys who see autonomy through the experience of sexual exploration.

What we see is that once again, for girls, there can be a sense of disconnection from the body and what goes on inside it – it remains alien and foreign. Adolescents become extremely self-conscious through the continual external emphasis on presentation, and how they appear to others. This leads girls to endless self-scrutiny and dissatisfaction with their body which links to low self-worth. The passive hostility experienced by some teenage girls towards their bodies is reflected in their tendency to tease and frustrate boys in a mildly sadistic way, but also to get involved in masochistic relationships with bullying, unavailable or even abusive boys. 'A girl can achieve vicarious mastery over her own sexuality by learning to manipulate a boy's passions, or by establishing psychological power and moral superiority over a boy who abuses her but desires her'(Cross 1993: 46).

Another aspect of sexuality and control – or lack of it – in adolescence centres around the longing for the experience of orgasm together with the worry that an orgasm will leave them even more out of control and vulnerable – opening up the possibility of the dissolution of the self.

Nicky, described in Chapter 3, badly wanted to find a boyfriend. When she wrote:

> The whirlwind of delight
> When I am at last yours
> And you are mine
> Together we'll be one

she was imaging the pleasures of safely losing herself in another in contrast to her actual sexual experiences where she felt denigrated and out of control.

Pulp's lyrics convey the confusion and the agony of sexual pleasure with the concommitant loss of control:

> What . . . is . . . this feeling called love? Why me? Why you? Why here? Why how?
> It's something I don't understand.
> And as I touch your shoulder tonight this room has become the centre of the entire universe.
> So what do I do? I've got a slightly sick feeling in my stomach like I'm standing on top of a very tall building.
> And I see flashes of the shape of your breasts and the curve of your belly and they make me have to sit down and catch my breath.

Worry about their sexuality, what to do, and with whom, and whether there will be anyone who will want to be involved sexually with them, is certainly a concern for most teenagers. These anxieties, as well as the concern about loss of control, are based on previous experiences and learned expectations about intimacy. As is described in Chapter 3, such sexual anxiety can lead to aggression, and sometimes to violence. For a boy those feelings are more likely to be released and directed outwards, in other words, someone else gets beaten up; for a girl the target for aggressive feelings linked to sexual anxiety is more likely to be her own body.

The body ego and image

In this section the mutual relationship between the body and the mind, and the implications of this relationship for self-harm, is explored. When Freud wrote 'The ego is first and foremost a bodily ego; it is not merely a surface entity, but is itself the projection of a surface' (1923: 26), he also emphasised that the ego was ultimately derived from bodily sensations, especially those coming from the surface of the body.

The development of the body image is hugely important in the process of the emerging sense of self. Processes of identification and internalisation of early object relations crucially relate to this development. Thus the sense of a skin which can consistently and dependably contain the child's body, with all its uncontrollable sensations and instinctual processes, is seen as being established through the combination of various elements in the maternal environment. These include eye contact with the mother, as a mediator of emotional containment and also, as Haag writes: 'tactile reinforcement of the child's sense of having a backbone' (2000: 7). In her paper on the construction of the body ego in infancy, Haag (2000) interestingly notes the different stages of the process of constructing the body image. Included in the third stage, around the age of 5 months, is the incorporation of the small and large joints of the limbs, which are experienced at a primitive level as links. She writes: 'In states of auto-erotic illusion the hand is the first representation of the breast. Contemplation of the hand-joint seems to be part of this auto-eroticism' (2000: 14). This is relevant both in the context of the earlier discussion on masturbation and the link with the mother's hand, but also in thinking about the location on the body of much self-cutting. From infant observation it is noted that the wrist-joint is a special object of contemplation, and is frequently a target for attack at times of unhappiness. It appears that there is a powerful attraction to the same location many years later.

In 'normal' development, pre-natal and the earliest of post-natal experiences of sound, touch, taste and sensation all contribute to a sense of the gradually developing experience of emotional consistency and integration. Over time the baby builds up an expectation of a response to her needs, and this leads to increasing confidence. There is a two-way process involved of projection and introjection – an intense form of communication gradually leading to identification and mental representation.

These earliest of experiences build up a coherent sense of the body ego and body image.

In adolescence the upheaval of all the body changes contributes to the sense of emotional dissonance. The body image becomes shaken, as does confidence and a sense of emotional and physical coherence. A number of adolescents feel that they hate the way their body is developing and how they look. They sense that it is their body that is forcing them to have sexual fantasies, and eventually to behave in a sexual way. In situations such as these there may be an unconscious fantasy that the body is the cause of all the pain and anxiety, while the expression of feelings becomes limited, especially for girls, to the circumscribed arena of the body. It can then feel easier to punish the body than go through the worry of trying to relate to another person. A critical superego, as discussed in Chapter 3, can function to punish sexual urges, so cutting serves as a displacement for an attack on the genitals (e.g. Friedman *et al.* 1972). Attacking the body releases the tension arising from internal states of mind – including sexual and aggressive elements which are 'evacuated' by cutting the skin and opening up the body.

My focus here is that the body is not only the first object for needs, drives and sensations, and used early on as a metaphor, but is used throughout life as an object for the expression of the internal impulses and emotions. After all, the body, with its associated functions such as eating and defecating, is the most convenient and easy object for representing or enacting psychic conflict. In other words, our bodies and what we do with them reveal what is going on in our inner world.

Separation

Separation from home includes separation from both parents, or the idea of both parents, whether or not the family lives together, and most adolescents experience a sense of loss and grief behind all the struggles to become independent. What is being left behind is childhood and the familiar routine, which at one time provided security and comfort. The adolescent is coping with the demand to be treated as an adult, alongside a conscious or unconscious longing to remain a child. As the adolescent moves towards relationships outside the family, he or she is usually able to see the parents as they really are, and this may be quite disappointing. Alongside the recognition of what has not been good enough is a powerful desire for the parents to change. Naturally in the letting go of the parents there is also the lament of 'why can't they understand, and be how I need them to be'. This whole experience of separation from home can be terribly painful and so some adolescents defend themselves from it by holding on to their childhood past.

Diana (whom I also write about in Chapter 5) felt very anxious about leaving home. She had experienced similar difficulties as a younger child, and now at age 19 these conflicts resurfaced. She became anxious whenever either of her parents was away from home, and found it difficult to go out or stay with friends. Sometimes she did not want to go to her college courses or attend appointments, but, as she told me, she would force herself. Diana wanted all the family to stay at home, and did not like anyone else visiting. On one occasion when her aunt and uncle came for lunch, Diana was furious because her parents were talking to them; so, refusing to eat lunch, she went to her bedroom and cut herself with a craft knife. Diana's separation anxiety – her need to cling, and, through this, control her fears about separating from home – eventually extended to the whole family, and was hostile in its coerciveness. Her refusal to eat seemed to be part of her separation anxiety and it seemed that her anorexia, her cutting and her hitting of herself were all ways in which she diverted the conflict back into her body.

Diana applied for more courses away from home. She said she was very frightened at the thought of leaving, but was aware that she needed to let go. She thought her parents were brilliant but also felt jealous and hostile towards them. She thought that they hated her, and was able to realise that this was partly her own feelings towards them. Diana was in a difficult position as, if she left her parents – especially her mother – she could no longer protect them from her imagined all-powerful wish to hurt and destroy them. Leaving them would also mean leaving them alone – an idea that in some ways was untenable to her. The solution was to turn the aggression on to her own body. Diana's fear of leaving home was rehearsed by her regularly deciding not to go out when invited by a college friend. She would agree to the invitation, and then become increasingly anxious about the arrangements over food and travel. As the time approached, Diana would become distraught and sometimes cut or hit herself. In the psychotherapy we talked a lot about her mixed feelings towards everyone in the family – especially her parents – and her dilemmas about leaving home.

Diana longed for her mother to love only her, and could not bear anyone else taking up her mother's time, including her father. She was resentful of her mother's work and other relationships, saying that her mother preferred being with anyone other than her. For example, when her grandmother was staying, Diana described her mother not talking to Diana at lunch, but talking to grandma in an easy manner. Diana then remembered how, when she and her mother had had lunch together the previous day, they had sat in silence watching the news. Whenever she felt her mother was involved in someone or something else Diana became upset and angry, and then cut herself.

In the transference I glimpsed aspects of the encaptive conflict. In one session Diana appeared anxious about how I was; when I did not reply she came over to me and, leaning forward, said in a fierce voice: 'NO – how are you.' My experience was of a powerful, intruding figure peering rather desperately into my face. When she sat down again, I commented on her anxious feelings about how powerful she might be, and she agreed, saying 'Well, I do drain people'. As the session progressed Diana's anxiety about how *she* was became clearer. It emerged that she had begun to feel out of control and therefore very small in the waiting room. She had arrived early, but her anger at being kept waiting had felt powerful. I was then the tyrannical, obliterating figure who left her feeling depleted and needy. Later in the same session when Diana became distraught at how out of control everything felt she began to rock in the chair, stroking her face with a jumper she had worn as a baby and which she carried with her all the time. When I commented on this very vulnerable part of herself, Diana responded fiercely: 'Stop thinking for me – stop taking over.' She then continued to rock and talk to herself in a repetitive monologue, which seemed to give her some comfort: 'I want to sit in my room, on my own and shut the door.' Diana needed to keep me and any thinking part of herself out.

In the therapy Diana asked how many other girls I was seeing; she spoke about wanting to be dependent and rely on me, but if she did, how would she feel when she had to leave me? She felt worried about getting too close to someone and being taken over by them, but also dreaded being one of many and so unimportant, and then feeling rejected. This concern highlighted her issues around the core complex, and the dangers of intimacy with, or dependency on, another. In one session Diana said she did not like the fact that I was in control of when we met and the timing of the sessions; she demanded to know whether I saw lots of people or only her, and was furious – shouting and tearful. I pointed out her need to feel important and central to me alongside her fear that we might become too close.

As the end of the therapy sessions approached, and Diana made plans about moving out of the area, she progressed from what had at times been a more dependent, sometimes rather idealised relationship with me, to fury with my inadequacies as she experienced them, and my failure to make her feel happier about herself. It seemed to me that the only way

Diana could leave both home and therapy was through the energy of her anger.

Her anxiety exemplified the movement between separation and clinging; one part of her wanted to be reunited and desperately hold on to her family, while another part – the part applying for courses and working so hard to get good results – desperately wanted to get away and separate from these hateful relationships. Diana was afraid of feeling abandoned, but also longed to escape from the overwhelming feelings evoked in her relationships, particularly with her mother. Her fantasy of fusion with an idealised mother who could fulfil her needs was revealed in the transference, and in her longing for unrealistic closeness with her mother – 'the fantasy of ultimate narcissistic fulfilment' (Glasser 1992: 496). As described earlier in the book, the core complex means that in turn the mother is imagined as relating only narcissistically, so therefore she is seen as being both overwhelming (avaricious) and indifferent and therefore rejecting. This appeared clinically in Diana's worries over my availability and her desire to both be my special patient and yet not be taken over by me. This configuration leads to annihilation anxiety which is defended against through narcissistic withdrawal into self-sufficiency and aggression. The mother's and, in the transference, my perceived indifference, led Diana to feel that the combination of withdrawal and aggression might be relieved by turning the aggression on to herself by cutting.

Her separation anxiety was compounded by the encaptive conflict. This was made up of a suffocating, possessive and avaricious part of herself involved in sadistic attacks on another part of her that wanted to break free. The conflict was revealed in her behaviour and in the transference relationship. Diana longed for intimacy but appeared captivated by an engulfing, obliterating internal object that sucked everything dry. This part seemed to be in competition with a depleted, hungry baby part of herself that longed to be taken care of. These conflicts were revealed as she repudiated and detached herself from her body, yet greedily demanded time and attention.

Diana's difficulty in separating, especially from her mother, was a characteristic of a number of the young women whom I saw for psychotherapy. Such separation problems can continue well into adulthood, and sometimes resurface once the younger woman herself has a daughter, but they have their origin in early infancy. The mother–infant exclusivity, when both are the same gender, contributes to an intensity and associated ambivalence alongside boundary confusion. When the woman becomes the mother of a daughter, she does and does not want her daughter to be like her. This ambivalence can affect feeding and emotional nurturing, and psychically there can be confusion and blurring both for mother and child over the distinction between them, and the fact that they are separate persons. The pre-Oedipal attachment continues for the girl, and other phases and experiences build upon this base. For example, in the Oedipal experience a girl does not turn absolutely from her mother to her father; rather the father becomes an important addition. The Oedipus complex is therefore inadequately resolved, and the girl is left with 'an ambivalent struggle for a sense of separateness and independence from her mother and emotional, if not erotic, bisexual oscillation between mother and father – between preoccupation with "mother–child" issues and "male–female" issues' (Chodorow 1978: 168). Mothers largely experience their daughters as doubles of themselves, 'a narcissistic projection of sameness', and it is this projection of sameness which makes differentiation difficult for women (Chodorow 1996: 161). One possibility is that the daughter comes to experience herself as an extension of her mother.

Friedman *et al.* (1972) note in their study of adolescents who self-harm that psychoanalysts generally agree that one of the crucial changes which has to take place if the individual is to achieve psychic maturity is 'the detachment of the libidinal tie from the original objects' (1972: 180). This detachment takes place through a similar process to mourning, and leaves the individual free to establish new relationships. In the Friedman study he and his colleagues found that their ten patients – seven girls and three boys – were unable to give up their deep and ambivalent attachment to their mothers, and became sad and depressed at the prospect. All felt strong feelings of love and hatred towards their mothers, and the impending loss seemed to be experienced both as a confirmation of their powerful aggression and a threat to gratification of their needs.

Another finding was that the adolescents in their research study were all very self-critical, seemed to have little confidence in themselves and were preoccupied by intense guilt. The authors suggest that it is these features which seem to have been established through narcissistic identification with their mother, which are then in turn attacked by the adolescent's rather severe superego. A suggestion that the patient's self-harm involved an attack on the internalised object, and that this object was invariably the mother, is worth noting. In other words, the threat of external separation from the mother who is both loved and hated led to an attack on the internalised mother figure. The study found that the aggressive feelings of the girls were directed mainly towards their mothers, while the fathers were experienced as less significant though often helpful and friendly. The girls spoke of a need not to give in to their mothers, who were experienced as powerful, frightening and threatening to overwhelm. Friedman suggests this is partly a defence against the regressive, passive, masochistic, homosexual wishes in relation to the mother.

I think it is also possible to see in the findings of the Friedman *et al.* study aspects of the encaptive conflict that I suggest lies at the heart of the urge to self-harm. Attacking the body becomes a way of dealing with anxiety and aggression. For some patients the cutting represents an attack on the undifferentiated and internalised mother figure. This is illustrated by Fonagy (1995), who describes a dream brought by a 23-year-old patient suffering from panic disorder, and with a history of anorexia and serious self-mutilating behaviour.

> In the dream, she was aware of a feeling of terrible tension which she could only relieve by opening up her veins and watching her blood flow. The blood ran in tributaries which joined up and made a river. The river became wider and wider and flowed into an ocean.
>
> (Fonagy 1995: 582)

Fonagy then recounts his patient's associations to the dream. These led to the patient's fantasy that her mother was living in her own body, and the realisation for both patient and analyst that the young woman experienced her mother as living within her skin.

Attacking the external body as a way of managing the fantasised mother inside emphasises the blurring of the boundary between 'inside me' and 'outside me', just at a time when a sense of boundaries is most crucial, and the idea of the self as separate and apart from the mother needs establishing. Cutting the skin gives expression to the need to cut the ties and sever the connection with mother. It establishes a sense of body edge, and gives the cutter a powerful sense of ownership of her own body and her own blood. Repeated cutting increasingly tethers the young woman to her body as the locus for the solution to problem feelings. Thus self-harm not only acts as a self-soothing comfort, but – as mentioned earlier – can develop into a form of perverted self-mothering.

Many mothers and daughters are able to successfully establish a supportive and yet separate relationship. However, a mother can enter into an ambivalent attachment with the need to keep her daughter close to her, while at the same time wishing to push her into the world. This can take the form of exaggerated concern or open hostility, leaving both mother and daughter uneasy about the effects of separation. The combination of over-involvement and then rejection leaves the adolescent girl feeling confused, for in some ways it replicates the very attempts at severance from mother that the daughter herself is attempting. One result may be for the daughter to emotionally, and in some cases physically, cling to mother, replicating an earlier phase during infancy when the very young child first experimented with leaving mother.

Serious difficulties are found with mothers who have some sort of narcissistic disorder, which leads to their treatment of their daughters and their daughters' bodies in a sadistic manner. This may even be overt, though not acknowledged. The behaviour is not realised by the child, who keeps the mother in an idealised place where she is seen as all-knowing and all-powerful, though not as a warm or comforting person. The mother fails to protect the child and is herself the source of pain: 'these patients have, through multiple dissociation, intrapsychically retained an archaic dependency, a sadomasochistic bond to the mother and environment while simultaneously having a precipitate independence' (Montgomery and Greif 1989: 30). Such people find it very hard to be alone, as there is no good internalised object in their inner world; instead there is a fused dyad – with self-inflicted pain acting as the other half.

One dreadful outcome of such relationships is that in a paradoxical way the pain from cutting itself comes to represent both mother and not-mother. It is a reunion with the mother because of the association with pain, but because of the external sensation on the skin the cutting establishes the separateness of the daughter. The task of the psycho-therapist is partly to act as a paternal function in the sense of interrupting the undifferentiated dyad of mother and daughter. The therapist can then be experienced as an alternative to this sado-masochistic bond. The patient can begin to identify the sadistic part of her own self as 'mother', and, following this, memories and feelings can become separated and then validated.

In general, fathers as potential rescuers of the child from the mother often seem to disappoint their children. This may be because they are emotionally or physically absent, or merely ineffectual. In turn, fathers may be reminded of their own experiences with a seductive and frustrating or overwhelming mother, and so lack the experience of straightforwardly confronting their children's developmental need with love. One father whom I spoke to said how blood, cutting, women's insides, too much food or not enough food, vomiting and taking pills were just not what men were interested in; instead they were more or less all the things men feared most – why would they want to, or indeed how could they take part in all this 'women's stuff'?

Abandonment

Separation can sometimes feel like abandonment and rejection. However, some of the young women seen for psychotherapy had actually suffered serious neglect and loss in their childhood. Their early relationships seem to have included experiences of physical neglect and lack of parental care, and the fantasies and unprocessed feelings about this resurfaced in adolescence and provided insight into what had happened. These young women showed little emotional investment in the idea of protecting themselves physically, and little interest in taking care of themselves. In that sense the neglect had become a way of being. Orbach (1996) suggests that internalised states of deprivation and neglect make it easier to let go of the body as there is less to lose in terms of pleasure and satisfaction with little sense of self-preservation.

Others who had lost a parent or been left by a parent appeared initially either to be dismissive of any emotional response to this, or, the opposite, to be haunted by it. In one way or the other there seemed to be an inner preoccupation with what had been lost or had not happened. There was a sense that those who had experienced prolonged separation from parental figures, and those who could not remember feeling special or loved by anyone as children, were the least able to control their self-harming.

Part of the confusion characteristic of an adolescent state of mind is that there often lies a feeling of abandonment beneath all the strong instinctual processes, together with a fear that the aggression will drive people away. The young woman feels cut off from anyone who can gratify her needs, and at the same time is frightened of being taken over by her own feelings of aggression. There can be actual feelings of isolation, or it may feel *as if* this is the situation. Several studies highlight the link between feeling abandoned and self-harming. Friedman *et al.* concluded that 'the experience of "abandonment" acts as a triggering-off mechanism in that it confirms the adolescent's fear of destroying the object and hence his source of possible libidinal gratification' (1972: 182). Woods, in his clinical account, confirms the association with loss and the desire to cut or hurt the body. He writes, 'Separation came to be seen as the trigger. Typically she would cut herself when alone immediately after a contact with someone was broken' (1988: 55). He notes the theme of loss in the patient's history. Immediate memories of losses acted as a screen for an earlier loss of parental care with the birth of a sibling. Biven, in his analysis of a self-harming adolescent boy, looks at the themes of object loss, particularly the boy's loss of his mother, and his early history which was marked by tragedy and chaos. Biven describes the boy's regression in terms of 'envelopment' (1977: 343), a term that conveys both a sense of separateness, and of containment and mothering. This state was represented by one of the boy's self-harming behaviours, when he used plastic bags over his head as a form of substitute skin.

In the description of my work with Diana, I noted that she would experience this sense of abandonment when her mother talked to another relative, or whenever either parent left the home. When she cut herself with the craft knife because her mother was speaking to her aunt and uncle, I understood that Diana was attacking her mother in fantasy as well as attacking her own body as a way of dealing with the anxiety and aggression induced by her mother's response, perceived as rejection. Diana's body represented the internalised mother, but was also an object 'worthy' of punishment in its own right in that it contained the aggressive intent. The following clinical example describes a young woman who had had little consistent parenting. She seemed engrossed in thoughts of family life, and what it might be like if she was able to live with her family.

Julie was referred with depression and cutting in her last term at school. The school doctor recommended that she have short-term psychotherapy (eight sessions) before leaving. Her childhood had been unsettled: as a baby she was with her parents; as a toddler she had been looked after by a family relative for several months when her mother was ill. Following her parents' divorce when she was age 3 she had little contact with her father, but remembered some good years with just her and her mother. When Julie was 6 her mother remarried, and had two more children. The family went abroad, and when Julie was 8 she returned to England to go to boarding-school. During some holidays she stayed with relatives, but over the summer she would fly back to her family. She had moved schools at 11 and again at 15, and felt she was always leaving friends behind. Julie talked a great deal in the sessions about her feelings of betrayal and loss when school friends turned against her. She would start to feel close to someone at school, confide in them and then find that they no longer wanted to be friendly with her.

A month before leaving school, Julie's mother told her the family was returning. Julie was full of mixed feelings about this – she was thrilled that she could live with her family again, but furious that her stepbrothers would not suffer as she did. She imagined all the wonderful family times ahead, and put on hold any thoughts of independence. All she wanted to do was to live at home again. Her pseudo-independence had taken her through childhood, and it was as if she needed to make up for what she felt she had not had. In eight sessions it was not possible to do more than try and understand with Julie her feelings of betrayal and abandonment, and how these might be experienced in the transference relationship. She saw that they arose with particular friends, and how they linked to her family experiences. It was difficult for Julie to hold on to all the mixed feelings – she had felt very depressed, but when she heard her mother was coming to England she was thrilled and very hopeful that everything would work out.

Julie's self-destructive actions – and those of all the other young women seen for psychotherapy – became a route from secrecy into the public realm. This was a way for them to find their voice. Julie needed to talk about what had happened to her and how she felt. The family code had been to just get on with it. Julie made full use of the eight sessions, writing down between the sessions what she felt and bringing some poems she had written.

Chapter 5

Reversing the process
From action to articulation

How do you work with someone who thinks they already have a satisfactory way of managing their distress? How do you establish a therapeutic
relationship with them, and together begin to explore the meaning of their
actions? How do you move from surface concerns to the underlying
conflicts? This chapter focuses on such aspects of the psychotherapeutic
process, beginning with some thoughts on the importance of the working
alliance with people who harm themselves, and including pragmatic
concerns around safety, privacy and confidentiality. This is followed by a
discussion on interpretation, on how to deal with silence, and on working
with dreams as one way of accessing the unconscious. In the second part
of the chapter the deeper concerns of the psychotherapeutic process are
discussed, and some ways of thinking about the necessary shift from
destructive behaviour to constructive thought.

The working alliance

The working alliance is the basis for patient and therapist to work together
– in other words, without the co-operation of the patient (and obviously
the therapist) with the therapeutic process, nothing will happen. At its
simplest level the working alliance means that the patient attends sessions,
and tries to let the therapist know about cancellations. This basic co-
operation can be difficult for some young people who are harming
themselves. For example, there may be a reluctance to regularly attend
sessions if the young person was told to by someone else who was worried
about their behaviour. A young woman may feel that she has no difficulties, and that the problem lies with her parents, friends or boyfriend,
who are interfering. She may just feel that she cannot be bothered; or as
one patient would later say to me 'I couldn't be arsed'; or something more
interesting turns up; it's hard to get out of bed; or she 'forgets'. Such issues

have to be explored at an early stage of the work, otherwise the patient will stop attending altogether. The therapeutic process will only begin to happen when some part of the patient is motivated to regularly attend sessions.

Another concern linked to the working alliance that has to be dealt with early on in the treatment are the basic rules of the therapy sessions: the length of the session, usually a fifty-minute hour; what happens if the patient is late; and an agreed arrangement for missed sessions. The patient may want to know how many sessions she has to attend, or whether she can come for as long as she wants and needs. Her expectations or wishes about this may be based on previous experiences with social workers and doctors, and at a deeper level derived from earlier experiences with her parents. A patient who has felt let down by her parents will find it hard to trust adults, even if they appear well meaning; others may distrust all those whom they see as authority figures. Flexibility is often acknowledged as a prerequisite in the work with young people, but the structure and regularity of psychotherapy sessions provides an important framework for those experiencing inner disorder.

Frequency of therapy sessions may be determined by factors outside clinical judgement. If a counsellor or therapist is visiting a school one day a week, then sessions obviously have to be arranged on a weekly or fortnightly basis. If a therapist is based in one centre, it may be possible to offer intensive therapy – two or three times a week. Factors such as team support, the quantity and variety of types of work, and the capacity of the patient and the therapist are all factors to be considered. There may be situations where a short-term model of between six and twenty sessions is preferable to open-ended work, or where work is curtailed by the patient's circumstances. If short-term work is the preferred model, there are certain general features that can be identified. One characteristic is that the therapist is active and direct, and clear about what is being offered from the beginning of the work. Another is that there is an agreed focus for the prearranged number of sessions, usually linked to present-day difficulties rather than past trauma.

A short-term model would not be the treatment of choice for those who are seriously acting out, or for those with addictions or serious mental health problems. However, if the patient can identify a focal problem in the first few sessions, and demonstrates the motivation to try and understand that problem, this is an indication of their suitability for short-term work. For example, a young woman who has begun cutting recently, has some concern about her problem, and within the first few sessions has some insight about her feelings and their link to recent difficulties would be appropriate for short-term work. This requires the person to be clear, motivated and reasonably rational about their behaviour.

There needs to be some conscious agreed alliance between a rational part of the patient and the psychotherapist in order to provide the basis for therapy. While this sounds reasonable, it can be difficult to establish a framework with people who are repeatedly attacking themselves, especially if they are adolescent. In fact it is not surprising that adolescents are sometimes seen to be unsuitable for analytic work, usually because of their propensity to violate the therapeutic structure. Some patients set out to defeat this structure using strategies such as aggression, avoidance, over-submissiveness or being overly compliant, 'pseudo-madness' and seduction. Often, however, there is another part of them that wants to be seen and understood. This part may be denied and only partly conscious, but the therapist needs to access this longing. It is this link which will provide the basis for the establishment and maintenance of the working alliance during the psychotherapy, and which will provide a framework for analysis of the transference.

There is disagreement over how much the working alliance is affected by the transference, and much discussion on the interrelationship between the working alliance, the transference and the real relationship. A helpful position is taken by Meissner (1992), who, in his exploration of the working or therapeutic alliance, emphasises the interaction to which *both* patient and therapist contribute. For example, the therapist's respect, consideration, courtesy, tactfulness and empathy, alongside the patient's trust, responsibility to take part, and empathy towards the therapist's attempts to understand, all help to establish and maintain the alliance.

Over the course of the therapy the transference to the therapist as an authority figure can change. Ideally the patient will become increasingly authoritative about herself, though she will have started off in the position of the one ostensibly needing the help and professional authority of the therapist. Included in this concept of authority are ethical considerations, and the intent of the therapist to accept and work with the patient's values rather than impose his or her own values on the situation. In other words, the patient's cutting can be initially accepted although not condoned as a coping mechanism. The aim would be to uncover and understand the meaning so that the symptoms become redundant.

Before exploring this process it is helpful to briefly discuss some real and rather pragmatic issues around safety, privacy and confidentiality. In a sense they are broadly linked to the working alliance, as they are part of the ethical responsibilities of the psychotherapist. Obviously in psychotherapy and counselling it is important to provide a safe place for the patient: a room where there will be no interruptions, no telephone calls and no one looking in through windows. Although this sounds obvious, in some settings, such as schools, or in youth and community work, it is surprisingly difficult to find or maintain a safe place. For example, when working in a rural child guidance department, it was difficult to make the room I was allocated for an occasional clinic look appropriate or inviting for young people. The sessions were held in a doctor's surgery in the only room apparently available, which was dominated by an immovable chiropody chair and equipment . . . after months of complaining, a better room was provided.

A schools counsellor seen for supervision experienced a similar problem. The counsellor was offered a different room in the school at each weekly visit – initially a storage room, then a spare classroom – before a suitable and appropriately sized room was made available for her regular use. However, as the door to the room had a glass window, there were difficulties with other children trying to peer in, and, despite a notice covering the glass and asking for no disturbance, the counsellor suffered frequent interruptions with students entering the room. We talked about these problems in supervision. It seemed the only answer was for her to lock the door, and she had to discuss with and explain this to each person when they came for their session. The young person coming for therapy may be highly self-conscious about the sessions, and worried about other people knowing that something may be wrong. It may feel easier for them if the room is unmarked and the building relatively anonymous.

Issues around confidentiality and the privacy of the treatment may be complicated – especially if the patient is under 16. If the counsellor or psychotherapist is working in the public sector or for a voluntary agency there should be clear guidelines about confidentiality, particularly when following disclosure of sexual or physical abuse. Counsellors for some voluntary agencies explain at the outset that if the person discloses abuse then the counsellor is required to take this further, and inform statutory agencies. If the psychotherapist is working privately and offering complete confidentiality, there may be situations where the young person is unprotected, and the psychotherapist is left carrying real concerns about the young person's safety.

This is a dilemma with all self-destructive behaviour, especially when threats of attempted suicide are made alongside repeated cutting. This is when one needs the potential back-up of a medical and psychiatric network, with good contacts for possible referral. After all, if one is continually worried about the actual survival of the person between sessions it makes therapeutic work extremely difficult. It may be possible to negotiate a contract with the young person, allowing contact, or work, with the parents. Another possibility is to agree with the young person when the treatment begins that the psychotherapist will make contact with the patient's doctor. In some voluntary and statutory agencies, the psychotherapist will be able to share his or her concerns with a supervisor or manager. If the young person is seen as a serious danger to herself, further steps may be taken to protect her.

For example, an 18-year-old was seen on an outpatient basis by a psychiatrist and nurse, and also attended a voluntary agency for counselling sessions. She would often arrive for her appointments both at the clinic and the agency and announce she had just taken a large overdose. She also repeatedly and seriously cut herself. The procedure arranged with her and all those involved was that she was either accompanied or instructed to go to the hospital immediately, where she was given an antidote or had her stomach pumped. It was clear from the outset that this patient was not appropriate for psychotherapy, and she failed to respond to the psychiatric treatment she was offered. As the seriousness and regularity of the overdoses increased, it was decided that she needed to be admitted to hospital with a view to receiving long-term treatment in a residential unit.

In this situation both the counsellor and the clinic staff found the worry that the young woman would succeed in her suicide attempts untenable. This made it hard for any treatment to proceed. As there was a good relationship between the clinic staff and those working in the voluntary agency they were able to share their concerns and an agreed procedure was drawn up. With hindsight this patient had become addicted to self-poisoning and its aftermath, and this prevented anyone from reaching to help her. Consciously she wanted to seek help, but her symptoms and lack of capacity for insight made this too difficult.

Analytic work is about exploring the unconscious conflicts and processes that lie beneath the symptoms. This approach means that the symptom is not the direct focus of the work and contrasts with that advocated by Levenkron, an American psychotherapist, who suggests that the therapist familiarise him or herself with each cut, burn or bruise, and give a recommendation as to how to treat it (1998: 77). This technique could be experienced by the patient as a direct and physical intrusion, and certainly seems a somewhat concrete way for the psychotherapist to hold the concern evoked by self-harm. It might also lead to gratification for the patient or clinician if the patient has either cut or not. The symptom can of course act as a way of avoiding a meaningful relationship with the therapist. If the patient talks endlessly about the cutting, this distances the patient and therapist and interferes with the transference.

Interpretation of the unconscious

We now turn to thinking about the psychotherapeutic process, and the way in which interpretation through the use of words makes something conscious which was previously unconscious, or pre-conscious in the sense of being almost accessible to the patient. The concept of the unconscious is not only central to psychoanalytic and psychodynamic work, but also to any meaningful work with people who harm themselves. It is understood to include psychological processes and mental structures that are influenced by our earliest bodily experiences, as well as feelings based on early and significant object relations which are formed both from fantasy and reality. These can be repressed, denied or sublimated. These internal object relationships develop early in life to supplant and make up for what has been experienced as inadequate in external relationships, and shape our future perceptions and reactions. The encaptive conflict is one such internal object relationship.

The unconscious is expressed in a variety of ways such as through our dreams and fantasies, and includes inadmissible and involuntary ideas which motivate behaviour. Most importantly, the unconscious will emerge in the transference relationship with the psychotherapist. Interpretation is the way these unspoken feelings can be brought to conscious awareness in the therapy. An interpretation reveals an un-expressed part of a communication, or translates a wordless metaphor into speech. The word 'interpretation' suggests a very specific profes-sional skill, but is at its best when it is capped by a further insight and understanding from the patient. Interpretation is tentative, and while there can be confidence in the appropriateness of an interpretation, certainty in interpretation is unattainable. Giving an interpretation is not about giving the 'real' meaning; rather it adds to what the patient has said, offering further shades of meaning and other points of view. Insightful interpretations emerge from somewhere between the conscious and the unconscious, and the psychotherapist needs to find that place before making links between past and present, and the conscious and unconscious.

In this context it is worth highlighting the valuable distinction made by Steiner (1993) between interpretations that he terms 'patient-centred', when the patient feels that he or she is being understood, and 'analyst-centred', which gives emphasis to the patient understanding and gaining insight. The distinction lies in the recognition of where the patient's anxieties and thoughts are focused, and what is most enabling, but he claims both are necessary for the patient's total situation to be understood. There are certainly times when a young patient who self-harms is ready to take on something that perhaps they have previously avoided, and this may lead to a development in their understanding of themselves, and there are other times when the essential experience is to feel understood and held by the therapist's response.

Getting below the surface

A common experience for those working with young people is that it is difficult to get below surface statements (for example, about home, college or social life) to reach the underlying conflicts. It may seem a hard task to get to the meaning behind the gesture. The patient may answer only in monosyllables, or say they 'don't know' or 'don't care'. It may be very hard for the patient to think about their difficulties and talk about them with the therapist. There are a number of reasons for this. There may be denial that there is anything wrong, or the patient may project all the difficulties on to others. Another part of the denial may be a sudden flight into health: that there had been a problem, but now everything is better. There may be an understatement of the problem: the patient says she just scratched herself, or did it once to find out what it was like, or burnt herself just for a dare. The young woman who is attacking her body can feel that she will be rejected, disliked or disbelieved if she tells you what she is doing and feeling. This might be spoken about directly: 'you wouldn't like me if you really knew what I was like', or 'if I told you everything you wouldn't want to see me again'. Reassurance is usually unsuccessful, as it is the underlying fear and conflicts that need to be explored and understood.

Another way that therapeutic contact can be avoided is through jokes and entertaining stories, or light dismissals of difficulties, which can be seductive and easy to join in as a way of avoiding painful issues both for therapist and patient. Another defence may be the pseudo-sophistication of the patient who has already had therapy, and speaks with knowing jargon about their 'inner child' and the 'victim part' of themselves. Common techniques are for a patient to yawn, to complain of boredom, or to suddenly need to go to the lavatory, or outside for a cigarette. Linda, who is mentioned in several vignettes, liked to bring bags of sweets into sessions and would sit sucking and chewing, and laughing at my interpretations of her behaviour – this was of course a form of acting out, and I discuss how useful her acting out turned out to be later in this chapter. Sometimes such interruptions and behaviour can precede an important issue, or the patient may not be able to continue with what she is speaking about, and needs time to think away from the psychotherapy.

Resistance will always be present in one form or another so as to avoid recognition of painful feelings, but it can be interpreted – sometimes successfully and sometimes not. With Linda I had to wait until she was ready to understand why she wanted to eat sweets rather than talk to me. It goes without saying that the ultimate resistance is when the young person fails to attend, or decides to stop coming to appointments. Analytic practice aims to explore, understand and analyse the defences, while respecting the patient's need for them. The important aspect is to try to speak about and make sense of what is happening, either with the young person or through one's countertransference.

Working with silence

There is a problem working with young people when they are silent – an issue that must have existed for as long as the method of free association itself. It can either be in the form of an inhibition of speech in general or as a difficulty specific to the treatment, where it emerges as constant or intermittent silence during the sessions. There may be embarrassment when a young person has little vocabulary, and has had little or no exposure to thinking about feelings. This is less common among young women, who on the whole have a wider vocabulary for their emotions. However, at a practical level it may be possible in some settings to use drawing, paints, sand play or games as methods for lessening the anxiety around speaking.

At a different level, the worry about speaking might be one of anxiety and mistrust of the therapist, or a fear about the implications of speaking. If the psychotherapy is to help, the anxiety needs to be reduced, and a rigid silence from the therapist will not usually resolve this, especially when working with an adolescent. Young people are often concerned about feeling judged or criticised, and if they have been self-harming they may expect to be 'told off' for their behaviour. They may experience the therapist's prolonged silence as critical or rejecting. However, by remaining silent the patient prevents the psychotherapist from interpreting content, for, if interpretations are made, they are inevitably focused on the silent defence. In this way silence is one of the most incapacitating modes of communication. It can help the patient if the therapist voices her sense of what the patient may be worrying about, and models putting feelings into words. Another possibility is to engage the adolescent in more neutral conversation as one way of building up trust. If a patient is silent for most or all of a session, the psychotherapist will tend to be left full of feelings. The feelings can belong to either or both the patient and therapist, and include straightforward annoyance and frustration at the failure to speak. At other times the patient's silence may hide a non-verbal communication, such as fear of the effect of speaking or the further exposure to suffering.

For example, Anne was often silent for large parts of the session. Dressed in black and with her arms and legs always covered up, she would sit stiffly on the edge of the chair as if holding herself together. In a session a few months after we had begun to work on a three-times-a-week basis, Anne appeared anxious and sat pulling threads from her scarf. She was very quiet but the atmosphere felt tense. She had not attended the two previous sessions – one had been cancelled, the other missed with no reason given. I had worried about her, concerned for her safety, and so, partly to alleviate this, tried to explore what she had been feeling, but Anne replied 'I don't know'. After a longer silence I asked Anne what she was thinking, and to my surprise she told me that she did go over and over in her mind what she was thinking – but then thought it sounded stupid. I suggested that she might worry that I thought she was stupid. Anne replied 'no – me', and was silent. After a while I wondered whether there had been people who had been critical like that. Anne said that her mum didn't listen anyway, but sometimes when she was with her dad she did say something, and then there was too much made of it, so she wished she hadn't spoken. I realised that this was of course a dilemma in the therapy. I felt enormous relief when Anne did speak, and this led to a tendency to weight her words with significance, partly so that she might feel encouraged to continue. What she was telling me was that this felt counterproductive.

In the transference, I felt caught between the mother who did not respond and the father who made too much of her words. This thought gave her some relief in that she eventually responded and said that sometimes, if she said things, bad things happened. When she had told an earlier therapist something she shouldn't have, all sorts of bad things happened – her period came back after months of not eating and she didn't want it, then her cat died, and her mother rang up drugged saying she'd been beaten up by her boyfriend, and all because of what Anne had said. Clearly she was worrying that bad things might happen if she talked to me, and I later spoke of her feelings of responsibility. Anne's response to my remark was 'it's been like that forever'.

Almost a year later, Anne confided that one of the reasons she did not speak was her fear of the power of her words. A similar fear is described by Angelou, who in an early novel *I Know Why the Caged Bird Sings* (1984) describes the weight of guilt following her experience and disclosure of child sexual abuse, and the subsequent murder of the rapist. She elected to remain silent, believing that her words contained the power to kill. Anne's situation was not dissimilar, in that she talked very little in the sessions, and only when I initiated our discussion. She eventually revealed that following sexual abuse, the perpetrator threatened that if she told anyone her mother would die. For Anne this was a terrifying threat, one which fitted with her own perception that she alone kept her drug-addicted mother alive. When she told a previous therapist in a residential unit about the abuse, social services and the police became involved, and this led to family upset and trouble. This had contributed to a deterioration in her mother's health, so, for Anne, the threat became a reality. Her strong fear, that I needed to understand, was that this would happen again.

Working with dreams

Some adolescents who find it hard to talk about their feelings do find it easier to talk about their dreams, and are interested in thinking about their dreams. Perhaps this feels less exposing or a more detached way to think about their difficulties, although ironically the dreams brought to therapy can be painfully revealing about inner conflict – including the encaptive conflict – for the dream material facilitates the approach to the unconscious. In Chapter 6, Diana's dream clearly reveals her encaptive conflict formation. Often there is little need for intricate dream work to unravel displacement or condensation, and the patient herself can begin to see how her inner world is represented in her remembered dreams. It is also possible to see psychic change if dreams are brought to the psychotherapy over time. Developments can be revealed both in dream content and the way the dreams are remembered, and spoken about by the patient. This was the case in the work with Mary, described in the following clinical material. We could both see the changes that were happening inside her through the dreams she brought to the sessions.

Mary, aged 15, was referred for cutting herself. At our assessment meeting she described, in such a quiet voice that I had to strain to hear her, that she felt low and guilty, although there were no reasons why she should be depressed. She was a pretty girl, very neat in her school uniform and looked young for her age. Mary told me that she had neither been beaten nor abused, her parents were not divorced, and she did not live in bad housing. She said that the cutting had begun a while back, but was only discovered when her mother saw that Mary had cut the word LIAR on her knuckles. Mary had also been cutting her arms which her mother did not know about. She felt she wanted to cut herself, and did not really wish to know why.

When she cut she felt neither pain nor relief – she just did it. She did enjoy the ritual around the cutting (discussed in an earlier chapter). She liked sitting in her room thinking about cutting and choosing what music to play. She said she felt she was a liar because she must be pretending to be depressed. When I asked her about psychotherapy, Mary said she did not know what to expect, there would be nothing to say. Her mother had told her about her own counselling for depression when she had been younger, but according to her mother there had been a real reason for her mother's depression which was to do with her housing situation. When I met Mary's mother at the assessment meeting she told me how upset and horrified she was about Mary's behaviour. She had removed Mary's supply of razors (though Mary later replaced them). Mary's father was working away from home so her mother felt she was carrying all the responsibility and worry.

Practical difficulties meant that it was possible to arrange only twelve sessions. It was also agreed that Mary's mother would meet with a colleague for support on a regular basis. In the first two sessions Mary found it difficult to think of what to say, she had no curiosity about her symptoms and appeared to have no language to express what she might be feeling. She was very polite to me and spoke about having no problems, and a good and conventional family life. The sessions felt heavy and dull, and seemed to last for a long time. The leaden, rather concrete feel contributed to an anti-thinking culture which pervaded the sessions. The only accessible feelings seemed those of relief for both of us when it was time to stop. Mary said she had nothing to say and remained silent, unless I commented or asked her direct questions that she quietly answered – usually with a 'yes' or 'no'. As one way of finding what might be going on in her unconscious, and as a way of encouraging her capacity to self-reflect, I suggested that she might like to bring some dreams to the therapy, and to my surprise Mary immediately recounted two dreams she had had that week.

In the first she was with some rough people from her school. She described one girl in particular with her careless clothes and dyed hair, and in the dream Mary said she was having fun. In the second dream Mary jumped out of her bedroom window, which was on the fourth floor, and flew through the air. Mary described it as like swimming, using the butterfly stroke; it was very hard work, but she could stay afloat and look down on all the gardens below her, which were bright and big like a huge jungle. In her associations to the dreams, Mary spoke of her rather restrictive friendships at school, all with what she described as 'good girls'. There was this wild girl whom she really envied, because the girl didn't seem to care. The second dream brought up the rather manic destructive elements in her behaviour, alongside a desperate wish-fulfilment to do something forbidden, possibly sexual, and away from home. The flying suggested some misguided omnipotence and warned me of her disturbance. In general her dream life revealed fantasies, and an imagination full of wildness, danger and colour. It showed also that with encouragement Mary had the capacity for thinking metaphorically. The dreams proved to be the way for us to establish some sort of thera-peutic relationship. It seemed that for Mary the dreams acted as an intermediary for us. I think she experienced them as a way of avoiding a more direct intimacy which could have been experienced as engulfing or intrusive.

While Mary was reluctant to speak directly about her feelings, she did talk a little about the dreams and what she felt about them. It seemed that through her cutting Mary was expressing a part of her that was longing to 'let rip', and cut through what she experienced as the rather anxious, suffocating atmosphere at home. Her inner object relations suggested a formation around a rather intrusive, overwhelming yet denying part of herself that meted out punishment for her powerful instinctual feelings of aggression and sexuality. As we had the opportunity for only short-term work, I decided to focus on this other side of Mary revealed in her dreams, a side that seemed so at odds with how she presented. One consequence of this was that Mary became less polite and nice, and opened up to feeling irritated and angry with her parents and sister. At home she quarrelled with her mother with whom she felt especially furious. She felt, unlike her brother, that she had to care and be responsible for her mother, especially when her father was away.

Over the remaining sessions Mary brought other dreams, often of a sexual nature. In one she told me she was sharing a big, shaggy jumper with Alan, a boy at school whom she fancied. He had his head through one end and she had her head through the other, and they were both laughing. She hoped, she told me, that he would ask her out, as she thought they would get on really well together. Her cutting had lessened, though Mary told me that she wished she had done it more seriously to begin with, as it would now be a statement about herself and who she was. In one session, Mary spoke in a dream-like way about all the patterns she could have made on her body with her razor. She spoke of her hero in the Manic Street Preachers who had cut himself and disappeared, and no one knew whether he was alive or dead. She also told me that she had finally been allowed to go to a concert, and had felt completely wild and free when she 'body surfed' over the crowd. I felt these musings were part of her confusion about her identity. This upsurge of adolescent rebellion seemed to link with the previous repression. She was also testing me out to gauge my reactions to these thoughts and to the experience at the concert. Would I respond with the same anxiety as her mother? Did she have to feel responsible for my well-being? In my countertransference I did feel some concern over Mary's cutting and this was confirmed in her associations to a further dream.

In this dream Mary said she had been on a racer bike that had gone completely out of control. Her understanding was that she felt excited, but not safe. As we explored the idea of the racer bike, Mary told me she was worried that she had got out of control with her cutting. She had decided to have one last go, and she had cut more deeply than before, all the way round the top of her arm. She felt both pleased and scared, and part of her pleasure was that her mother did not know what had happened. In the transference I was the mother who needed to know about the cutting, and so work with Mary in helping her to understand and contain these mixed feelings of pleasure and fear. The dream of the out-of-control bike suggested that Mary's ego was not in charge of her aggressive and sexual impulses. The concern I had registered was partly a projection of Mary's concern about herself.

As we were working with a limited number of sessions I felt that Mary could be helped by a more directive style. Thus, later, when Mary spoke about her longing to make a noise at home without being criticised, we discussed her idea of joining a school-based rock band where she would sing some of the songs she had composed over the weeks of her therapy. The songs were based on the dreams she had had and her feelings about the dreams. In the next session, Mary said she wanted to show me her arms and told me she had not cut since our last meeting. She said she had decided herself not to cut again, partly because she felt less depressed, and partly because it was summer, and she wanted to wear short sleeves.

In her final session Mary brought a dream of a waterfall. She said that it was a big one and at the top it was very smooth and calm. In the middle it was wild, but you could get down to the bottom pool, where it was beautiful, with green water and some rocks, and it was calm enough for goldfish to swim in. Mary said herself that she thought she was a bit like the waterfall, with all these bits in her, and I suggested that she had brought all these different feelings to the therapy. On the surface she seemed smooth and calm, but underneath she had wild and worrying feelings which could suddenly feel out of control; these two parts led to an interesting pool with rocks and fish, full of colour.

From surface to depth

Using Anna Freud's (1969) statement that the psychotherapeutic process is systematic in its move from surface to depth as my starting point, I will now explore the move from self-destructive attacks on the surface of the body to talking about inner feelings. It is a theme of this book that the suffering body acts as an instrument or representation of unconscious communication; that the goal of therapeutic work is to translate this suffering into conscious communication, so that understanding and insight is gained. Part of the necessary shift from surface to below the skin involves a move from acting-out behaviour to acting in, in the sense of bringing the conflicts to the therapy. Part of the necessary shift from action to articulation lies in enabling the patient to think about the function and meaning of her self-harming behaviour, what it represents and how the urge to damage herself can be managed in other ways. In a similar way, the psychotherapist helps the patient who harms herself move from concrete actions to metaphoric thinking. In the final part of this section, I discuss the resurfacing of a form of infantile omnipotence – a characteristic of those who harm themselves. Alongside the quest for omnipotence is a concomitant fear of death.

From acting out to acting in

The analytic task was originally seen as relatively straightforward, for, in his early writings, Freud (1895) thought that the patient would become free of symptoms once they had been spoken about. As his work developed, Freud found that the move from passive symptoms to active speech and insight was a more intricate and complicated process involving repetition, often through transference, remembering and working through (1914). As has been explored above, a reasonable working alliance was a necessary prerequisite for this process to occur. For Freud acting out was seen as part of the remembering, a reproduction within the transference, not as a memory but as an action (1914: 150).

The concept 'acting out' developed from this early formulation, and in 1968 Anna Freud acknowledged that there was confusion about the concept, and accepted that it had widened to describe experiential attempts at re-enactment or enactment in the clinical situation. More recently it can also be seen as behaviour that happens while the patient is in therapy but away from the sessions. It may be seen as a form of communication and a precursor to the patient thinking about the behaviour. I am using the term here to include all behaviour relevant to the psychotherapy – whether in sessions or outside.

Acting out is one of the characteristics of an adolescent state of mind – it is what adolescents or those in an adolescent state of mind do. Tonnesmann quotes Blos (1963) who sees it as serving three different aims. In the first it serves as a conduit for the unconscious motivation of the young person's parents; second, its purpose is to manage tension raised from conflict anxiety; the third aim is to protect the psyche from the anxiety caused by an experience of structural disintegration or inner fragmentation (Tonnesmann 1980: 27). Most of us who have worked with young people recognise the difficulty in being able to calmly differentiate sudden and unexpected mood swings and dramatic upsurges of emotion – the 'whatever is going on here' experience. As noted, there is often a tendency for action or acting out to be one of the dominant means of communication, and Tonnesmann makes the helpful comment that as therapists 'we have to offer ourselves more often than not to be "acted-out" on' (1980: 34). In other words, the adolescent requires somewhere for this 'acting-out on' and an appropriate someone who can meet this need. There is however benefit for the psychotherapist as the acting out is one way of gaining a sense of the patient's internal world and inner object relations. It gives us a sense of the psychic conflict, and how past trauma is experienced in the present. It is also a means of communication, and, helped by the therapist's constructions and reconstructions, can be a route to understanding.

Linda was mentioned earlier in this chapter for her tendency to come to sessions with bags of sweets – also a form of acting out. This alerted me to her infantile longings with her noisy chewing and sucking. Linda laughingly dismissed my interpretations of her need for comfort as rubbish. I think she was also frightened of what might emerge in the sessions, and wanted to fill her mouth with sweet things in case I gave her something she did not like the taste of to chew over. She ignored my interpretations of her laughter as a way of managing all the painful feelings. Interestingly Linda's mother was involved in the confectionery business, and I understood Linda's clutching and holding on to the sweet bags as an acting out of her longing for her mother's nurturing.

Indications of the same early deprivation further emerged when for a few months she brought with her to her sessions a little girl, aged about

3, whom she child-minded. There was no initial discussion about this; Linda just arrived for her session with the child – the option was either no Linda, or Linda plus child. The dynamics evoked provided enormous insight and understanding of Linda's early experiences. Initially I was the one who felt put out and disoriented – the usual format was changed, and I had to provide some toys and colouring materials, and move the plants from the window-sill. These feelings gave me a sense of Linda's own displaced feelings from her childhood, when a much loved and wanted sibling arrived. In the sessions Linda paid no attention to her charge – she said she wanted to talk to me, and became upset and furious when I had to respond to the child as she tried to climb on to the furniture and took my attention away from Linda. She said the child should just get on with it, and we were both able to link this to Linda's own felt experiences. We had to talk together about how to manage the sessions, and Linda's feelings of being excluded and deprived of my attention. Unconsciously, Linda had brought the child as a way of avoiding the increasing transference relationship, which brought with it her anxieties about both rejection and engulfment. Once we both got to grips with this, Linda managed to arrange for a friend to look after the child while she had her sessions. The strong feelings she had experienced with me helped us both understand a great deal about Linda's past and present difficulties.

In this second example the acting out was less accessible to interpretation and became increasingly uncontrollable and worrying. Angie, an apparently street-wise 20-year-old, appeared highly motivated when she was referred following an overdose, hitting herself and a problem with drug use. At the assessment interview she was very lively and talkative, telling me and my colleague all about her history and her memories of attending child guidance as a young child. We decided that she should come for psychotherapy, but that she would also be invited for a monthly meeting with the consultant psychiatrist. Before her second session she rushed into the waiting room, leaving brightly coloured messages on the blackboard exhorting other children to keep going and survive; she then told me she could never go into the waiting room again, and in future would have to wait for me in the hall. This provided a way for Angie to describe how she felt forced to go to a child guidance clinic as a child, and how she felt she was expected to be upset about her mother who had left shortly after Angie's second birthday. She was upset and longed to be close to her mother, but as she explained she had had ongoing contact with her mother over holiday times, and some people did not have parents at all. The acting out in the waiting room alerted me to what Angie was not telling me, which was her underlying concern that coming to sessions might prevent her from keeping going or even surviving. At some level Angie felt that she had had no parents, and that in her mind 'being forced to have feelings' about this was dangerous.

Angie talked and moved about throughout her sessions. The effect on me of the sound and movement was that I found it hard to retain the content of her outpourings, but was moved by an accompanying feeling of emptiness and deadness. Angie always wore brightly coloured clothes and changed her hair colour for each session. Her arms were tattooed with intricate designs, alongside a tiny heart with the word 'mother'. Her adolescence had been very unsettled, and had included living with her father and his new girlfriend, moving to her grandparents, followed by some time in care. Over the time we met, Angie lived in several shared houses with different friends; she was never settled and was uncertain about the future.

When I attempted to reflect on what she told me and interpret, Angie would respond with pop psychology phrases or New Age clichés, and I realised that it would be difficult, and perhaps inappropriate, to get beyond her highly defensive stance. Angie was very anxious about establishing a meaningful relationship with me, and employed different forms of acting out to avoid this. She told me that she had had a good relationship over a number of years with a social worker. They had ended up friends and still corresponded, though Angie found it difficult that they no longer met, following Angie's move out of the area.

Angie often acted out, revealing her anxious defence against the transference – she would turn up late, or at the wrong time, or on the wrong day. On one occasion, our fourth session, she arrived very late and stoned. I did not realise how far she was under the influence of drugs until she sat in my room. With hindsight it might have been more appropriate to have rescheduled the session, but I worried about sending Angie away. I thought she would experience it as rejection no matter how carefully I phrased it. The brief and unsatisfactory session consisted of my interpreting her state as linked to her anxiety about intimacy, and her need to keep me away and sabotage the therapy. In response Angie yelled and howled with laughter, only stopping to point out to me that one of the plants in the room looked as if it were dying – this, she added, was no way for a therapist to treat her plants. On her way out Angie said that as a child she didn't turn up for her child guidance, she just wouldn't go, but now she turned up stoned.

I think that by acting out in this way Angie confirmed her vulnerability, and her fear that my words might seem like ill-treatment and kill her off in the same way that she perceived the plant. Her internal world seemed fragmented and confused, and there were no good internal objects present. At one level she wanted to talk about her childhood and her mixed feelings about her parents, at another level she was terrified by the strength of feelings and weight of the loss and separation from her mother. In terms of the encaptive conflict she appeared dominated by a threatening, punitive figure who might obliterate Angie through neglect, yet to cut free from this figure would leave Angie with nothing. This session confirmed for me my doubts about Angie's suitability for psychotherapy. She had little reliable external support in her life, and was attracted to risk-taking and impulsive behaviour.

Angie stayed for a few months before moving away to another town with a new boyfriend. Over the remaining sessions I offered support to her in her attempts to get a job and stay away from destructive relationships. When she talked about the past and present I listened to her feelings about it, but did not encourage the transference. Angie did not come stoned to a session again, but still continued to be late or to turn up at the wrong time. In this situation the acting out, as well as revealing Angie's past trauma, was a communication that confirmed for me that supportive therapy was more appropriate than psychoanalytic psychotherapy, and that I needed the back-up of the consultant psychiatrist in case Angie took another overdose.

From self-harming to self-reflection

Some people find thinking about feelings problematic, and yet psychotherapy is a talking cure which places emphasis on verbal symbols – 'words', rather than physical symbols – 'wounds'. Earlier in this chapter I discussed how dreams can be used, and how the visual images from a dream can be verbalised. In younger children play is as symbolic as words and can be used to interpret psychic conflict. The cutting is both symbol and symptom, and a defence against the underlying psychic conflict. For some young women self-harming is easier than self-reflection, as they find thinking about what they might be feeling a fearful and empty prospect. Young patients can find it easier to describe the external events leading up to the attack, and through this start to gain some insight into the conscious reason for cutting. They might also want to describe their feelings after cutting. A more difficult part of the thinking is to try to understand what lies behind the behaviour, and how the act is represented or symbolised in the internal world.

In this context Fonagy's (1991) work on thinking (briefly discussed in Chapter 3), and the aptitude to represent mental events, is extremely valuable. He notes that this ability, whether conscious or unconscious, is frequently referred to in the context of the capacity for symbolisation. He prefers the term 'mentalize', and notes that the 'capacity to conceive of the contents of one's own, as well as the object's mind, is an important requisite for normal object relationships' (1991: 649). In other words, in the context of self-harming, if the patient is to relinquish the behaviour, she needs to be able to represent the cutting as equivalent to a feeling state or a sensation, namely to mentalize her own feelings and thoughts. To be able to think about one's own feelings and what the other person might be feeling is necessary for normal relationships. Unfortunately for a number of people this ability is impaired, and Fonagy is also helpful for an understanding of this deficit.

He explains that the development of the ability to self-reflect on one's own and others' feelings is dependent on the presence of adult models, whose mature egos can provide a framework for the formation of these structures within the child. These same structures then help to establish boundaries for the self. The developing child is seriously impaired if the adults around are unable to provide the necessary conditions for the establishment of such structures. 'We may expect deficits of mentalizing capacity in cases where traumatic events concerning one or other of the parents compel the child defensively to disregard perceptions related to the thoughts and feelings of the primary object' (1991: 650). Some children may never, or can only partially, learn and internalise this capacity. For others the ability to think about feelings becomes blunted and tarnished by cumulative traumatic experiences, and their sensitivities are dulled and invalidated. One of the ways this capacity can be developed, repaired and internalised is through the therapeutic relationship, when the therapist becomes a model of how to reflect and think about feelings.

In this context it is important to return to the concept of dissociation. This was discussed earlier as a specific, adaptive and dynamic response to severe trauma, which serves to alter the sense of personal identity so that emotional distress is avoided. These defences, which act as a form of protection, can of course re-emerge whenever the person feels threatened. One of the effects of dissociation is that the unbearable feelings from infancy which were unthinkable remain unthinkable, as the person has no symbolic mental representation of what happened, and limited experience to creatively use their imagination. Bion (1967) noted that in dissociation an attack on linking between perception and thought, feeling and image, sensation and thought takes place. This can lead to what McDougall (1986) describes as 'alexithymia', a state of mind where patients have no words for feelings, and as a result are 'disaffected'. It is in these sorts of states of mind that people can either harm themselves and experience no pain, or harm themselves in order to feel pain. To reconnect, the person has to begin to imagine and create some way of representing their sensations, feelings and perception so that this can be thought of, recognised and integrated.

The example that follows shows how hard it is for some young people to mentally represent and verbalise their distress. Lucy, an 18-year-old discussed in an earlier chapter, was seen for weekly sessions following an overdose and cutting of her upper arms. She also sometimes felt a bit faint, though the doctor had put this down to the anti-depressants that he had prescribed for her. Lucy was an attractive, solid-looking young woman who lived with her mother, and she told me when we met that her father had left when she was about 2 years old. She had had some contact with him, but he lived abroad. Making contact with him was discussed in Chapter 2. Lucy's mother was also on anti-depressants, and Lucy said she both felt sorry for her mother and fed up that she was so bad-tempered. Lucy found it very difficult to think about how she felt, except that she felt hard done by. The sessions were filled with Lucy's complaints about her lack of money, her boredom, her friends who let her down and the selfishness of her entire family. She said that she did not really know why she had taken the overdose, and that she cut herself for something to do. In my countertransference I felt disconnected from the experience of being with her. The sense of emotional flatness pervaded the sessions – there was no obvious affect. She was pleasant to look at and I found myself drawn to share her fantasy that there was no point in thinking about it all, other than at this superficial level.

However, over time it felt as if upsetting feelings were beginning to surface. Lucy's complaints remained the same, but I noticed that the texture and atmosphere of the sessions began to subtly change. Lucy had no curiosity about what she might feel alongside her complaints, but I was curious to see that during sessions her skin, as revealed on her neck and lower arms, became red and covered with small lumps. This extended to the side of her face, and when Lucy began to scratch herself I suggested that something seemed to be bothering her. Lucy laughed and said that both she and her mother came out in such rashes; her mother would laugh about it, and dismiss it as a family characteristic. It had always happened, but she could not understand why it should happen in the therapy when she was just sitting talking with me.

I suggested that perhaps there were feelings just below the surface that were bothering Lucy and making her feel uncomfortable and itchy.

Perhaps they were not to be laughed at; rather we needed to take them seriously and try to think what the reddening skin and lumps might mean. Lucy became interested in how seriously I took the rash, and this somatic manifestation gave us a chance to think together about how upset she might be about her mother. The sensation from the rash was so irritating that it could not be ignored. I suggested that although Lucy was telling me one thing, she might be feeling a great deal more inside. Lucy still did not know what she might be feeling – she was irritated by the rash and how unsightly it looked. It was easier to have the rash, despite the itching, than to recognise her feelings. In the same way it was easier to cut herself than think about why she felt the way she did. Both the itching and the cutting were wordless metaphors representing her underlying feelings. This experience helped Lucy to start to try and think about herself in a serious way, and she began to acknowledge that at times she did feel very upset, sad and angry, though at this stage she did not know why. The red rash Lucy shared with her mother suggested that Lucy was struggling to separate from a mother who had got under her skin, and from whom she could not differentiate herself. The encaptive conflict involved internalised aspects derived from this over-involved relationship with her mother.

In this example I was working with someone who found it really hard to think about feelings, other than the most ordinary complaints, and yet clearly she was very confused and unhappy. Lucy had no real sense of why she was feeling as she did, and could not begin to think about it. Her body was showing her distress, but prior to the itchiness and lumps emerging her feelings had seemed unreachable. Lucy did not know what she felt, she could not link sensation to thought. With hindsight the regular sessions were beginning to bring Lucy more in touch with her feelings especially about her parents, but as there was no verbal route these feelings emerged through symptoms – physical symbols. Perhaps Lucy exchanged the previous symptoms of cutting and overdosing with the eruption of the itchy lumps in the sessions. I think the fainting was also demonstrative of her inner disintegration and rage. Her body collapsed, and when she took the overdose Lucy wanted to die. Lucy experienced a sense of hopelessness in sustaining herself, and wanted to deny the mess inside. The somatic manifestations showed how psychologically damaged Lucy was, and gave a sense of some internalised mother and baby frustrations.

From action to metaphor

In moving from surface to depth there needs to be a shift from concrete action to an awareness of the symbolic meaning that lies behind the action; in other words, an awareness of the metaphoric function. One particular characteristic of ego functioning that can be found in therapeutic work with people who are attacking their bodies is the 'thing-like' quality of the destructive behaviour. In this I include the ritual, the objects used, the very way an incident happens – all these can have an unusually fixed and unalterable quality. It is this quality that is brought into the consulting room when the young person describes her behaviour: 'this is what I do' and 'what you see is what you get'. The self-harming action sometimes equates to an actual immediate trigger experience, and, in the mind, serves a 'real' function through its enactment. In this situation it is difficult to gain a sense of any feeling or fantasy around the act, or any imaginings or memories. Such a characteristic can be defined as 'concretism', but may at times seem almost psychotic.

This concrete quality is well illustrated by the account given by Bollas of cutting by a patient whom he refers to as 'S':

> My cut is secret . . . I slice my skin with a fine razor . . . I place one cut next to another, each a valley of incisions. . . . Up it flows, up and out, spilling over my skin. Pure. No effluence of eggs. No dead babies here.
>
> (Bollas 1992: 138)

Bollas' patient 'S' equates the cuts she makes on her skin to the 'cut' of her vagina, or as she describes it 'cunt', with the 'n' crossed through.

This can be seen to link to Freud's (1915) discussion of thing-presentation and word-presentation with his more disturbed patients. Freud writes of the predominance of what has to do with words over what has to do with things; it is this that contributes to the strangeness of the substitutive formation in schizophrenic symptoms. Thus in the above extract there is only a slight similarity between cutting an arm with a razor and a menstrual period, and, to paraphrase Freud, still less similarity between the surface of the skin and the deep bleeding from the uterus. However, in the former case there is, in both instances, 'a spilling out', while in the latter the cynical saying 'a hole is a hole' is true verbally. As Freud writes:

> What has dictated the substitution is not the resemblance between the things denoted but the sameness of the words used to express them.

When the two – word and thing – do not coincide, the formation of substitutes in schizophrenia deviates from that in the transference neurosis.

(Freud 1915: 201)

Segal (1957), in a seminal work, notes the relationship between disturbances in symbol formation and the development in the ego and its way of dealing with its objects. In concrete or 'schizophrenic' thinking, the lack of difference between the thing that is symbolised and the symbol is connected with early disturbance in object relations. The process she suggests is one of projective identification, where internal objects and parts of the ego are projected into an object which is then identified with. The resulting confusion obscures any differentiation.

Young women who harm themselves are not usually schizophrenic, but there is at times a quality of strangeness to the accounts of their actions. This strangeness is sometimes reflected in the emotional flatness of the sessions and the accounts of such sessions, which could link to the experience of dissociation – the cutting has taken place at a level of 'one remove' and on the 'alien' body. As noted above, the work is to help the patient re-establish the connection between what they see and feel with thought, and to develop the capacity to symbolise and mentally represent feeling states. In this way the concrete actuality of mental constructions can be overcome.

I would not want to minimise the experience of the survivors of the Holocaust by making a facile comparison with the experience of self-harming young women, but I do think that the findings of Grubrich-Simitis can be usefully employed in other, less horrifying contexts. In her work with Holocaust survivors Grubrich-Simitis explores the impairment of the ego function of metaphorisation as a result of the Holocaust trauma. She describes how, under such dehumanising conditions, behaviour became totally determined by primary needs of self-preservation; it became unambiguous, with little room for the use of fantasy and for 'as-if' behaviour (1984: 306). Using this idea it does seem that for some of the young women there was an impairment in their ego functioning from the early mother–baby relationship affecting their thinking capacity. This impairment can also be an inhibition of thinking, so there is a pact of silence that surrounds an original traumatic experience. This can be a trauma, such as sexual abuse, experienced directly by the young person when a child, or an experience that actually belongs to their parent's childhood – a transgenerational transmission of trauma (Gardner 1999). A further reason for such an impairment could link to the state of adolescence itself with its throw-back to an earlier infantile state. Here there is, at times, serious erosion between internal and external reality, past, present and future, and self and object representations – external and internal security may feel at a minimum.

Why is metaphor so necessary? The obvious reason is that through the use of metaphor the young person can express feelings and impulses without having to perform dangerous and risk-taking actions. For example, through metaphor, aggressive and murderous feelings can be expressed without suicide or murder taking place. It is not simply to do with talking rather than acting out, but because it is clear that the word is not 'actually' meant. In metaphoric use the word is not used literally, hence the idea of the 'as-if' quality. For this usage to develop, the therapist and patient first have to become aware of the awfulness of the patient's experiences and the way those experiences have been internalised.

The very process of analytic work with its emphasis on dreams, signs and symbols can begin to work as a form of modelling for thinking metaphorically. In this way the young person can begin to experience thinking, not through pseudo-metaphorisation, but through a new experience with the psychotherapist. Both interpretation of the transference, and the experience of the psychotherapist as a 'new object', can contribute to the development of the patient's imagination. The patient who is trapped in concretism cannot actually imagine, but if this begins to shift then the transference is a further way of developing the idea of metaphor.

From omnipotence to self-esteem

In this final reflection on moving from surface to depth, I discuss a necessary shift within the person which is to do with their belief in themselves. My contention here is that however the body is attacked, it implies a belief in omnipotence. The attack is a paradoxical gesture made in a state of false consciousness, and needs to be replaced by a genuine sense of self-esteem and self-worth. Such omnipotence is characteristic of an adolescent state of mind, and can become inflated through a false belief both in invulnerability and control of body changes and psychic conflict through physical destruction. Though fuelled by desperate anxiety and upset, taking control of one's own self-destruction is a powerful and exciting activity.

It appears that the longing for omnipotence and taking destructive control is in inverse proportion to the deep insecurity and fear of annihilation. Ultimately the desire for omnipotence is linked to the fear of death and equated with separation, and dark, helpless and vulnerable feelings. Omnipotence and fear of death are part of the infantile experiences revisited in the adolescent mind-set, and link to attacking the body.

An intriguing expression first used by Pumpian-Mindlin and quoted by Greenberg (1975) is 'omnipotentiality', a state manifested during late adolescence. In it the young person (in this writing referred to only as 'he') is convinced that he can accomplish any task, physical or intellectual, or solve any problem, despite finding it difficult to complete any one thing. The resolution of this phase comes about from acting out omnipotential fantasies and submitting them to reality testing. Linked to this is also the attempt to recapture the lost omnipotence of childhood, 'the belief in totally effective control over one's inner and outer world, at the very moment when basic security is threatened by psychological distancing from the objects, and the concomitant awareness of the certainty of personal death' (Greenberg 1975: 233).

Both states lead to this false consciousness and belief in control and power, though a gender perspective on the phase of omnipotentiality might suggest a different emphasis for late adolescent girls who are attacking their bodies. At one level some of them struggle with issues of learned helplessness, and feel that they do not have the potential to achieve anything or go anywhere. Others are overly defensive, and appear to have a powerful belief in their ability to deal with everything that life throws at them. Underneath there is a passive, regressed, almost masochistic belief in what will happen to them and this can lead to a 'pseudo-omnipotence' manifested through symptoms such as cutting which appear to offer control both over their external body and inner thoughts.

The task of the psychotherapist is to try to understand at the same time as exploring the destructive and damaging attempts to take control and feel powerful. The pseudo-omnipotence needs deconstruction, so that the patient can gain insight into the origin and needs behind her self-harming. The effect will be to help the patient separate and develop autonomy, which in turn leads to an increase in self-worth and self-esteem. As a final comment, the feelings of being separate and apart from parents are usually offset by a strong need to be part of a group. As is well known, groups of friends help the adolescent define herself through connection with others, but the adolescent who is excluded or excludes herself for being different is further isolated, and at risk of using self-harming for self-definition and self-satisfaction. In such situations alongside the sense of omnipotence, and conflated with the wish to self-harm, there may be contempt for being ordinary or being like everyone else. This frame of mind is illustrated in the following clinical description.

Jade was 19 when she was referred following illicit drug use and risk-taking behaviour which included some self-injury. Jade had gone abroad in the summer, back to a country where she had lived as a small child. Up until this holiday Jade had experienced no apparent difficulties, fitting in well both at home and school. Once away, she had become attached to a group of people involved in drugs and drug dealing, had been involved in a car crash, and had suffered some sort of breakdown. Jade's father had fetched her home, and both parents, although divorced, were concerned about their daughter.

When I met Jade she was full of stories about what an amazing time she had had over the summer, how many different types of drugs she had experimented with, and her opinions about them. She talked about the characters she had met, their crazy ways and unconventional life-style. She told me how excited and afraid she had felt as they had driven around the country, and all the occasions when they had nearly been killed by drug dealers. Jade had been seriously out of her depth, but was full of contempt for her English peers and their restricted social life, and for how small and drab England was. She felt she had outgrown all her local friends and badly wanted to return abroad, where she felt special and part of an important group. Jade's false confidence and bravado belied her terror at the experiences she had had.

In the psychotherapy sessions she did not want to think about the withdrawal and isolation that had apparently preceded the breakdown, which she dismissed as to do with a particularly heavy load of drug taking. She did not want to think about her parents, who infuriated her, nor about the feelings she might have had following their difficult divorce eight years previously. Jade dismissed her mother as feeble and selfish, and her father as controlling and absent. In the sessions Jade either sat yawning, complaining of boredom, or recounting tales of violent drug dealing among the drug barons she had met, while checking to see if I looked shocked (like her parents) or impressed (like some of her friends).

Two months into the weekly sessions, Jade began to seem a little less inflated and defensive, and began to talk about her father's affair and subsequent leaving home. In his new relationship he had become stepfather to two girls, both slightly older than Jade. It became clear that Jade regarded herself as small and drab compared to these two apparently attractive, confident and successful stepdaughters. They had been to university, travelled abroad and had lots of boyfriends. Jade felt envious and hostile towards both of them, and was determined to cope with these feelings of inferiority by showing how unconventional and extraordinary she could be. Her hatred towards her father for leaving, her mother for letting it happen, and towards her father's new partner and her two stepsisters had been expressed through the risk-taking behaviour, the brushes with death and her family's worry about it all.

Despite some sessions where it felt as if Jade was prepared to think about her feelings, and her need to take risks and harm herself, she decided after a few months that there was no point coming to therapy and that she would much prefer to live abroad. The therapy ended after an agreed final session. It had not been possible to change Jade's feelings of omnipotence to feelings of self-esteem, nor understand her attraction to, and fear of, death.

Thinking about this encounter in retrospect it was clear that Jade could not bear to see herself as ordinary. She needed to believe that she could cope with everything, and in that way was special and different from her stepsisters. Inside, Jade did not feel that she had been seen and responded to as special. In her experience her father was attractive but abandoning, and imposed his authority, while her mother was self-absorbed and vulnerable, and Jade did not want to be anything like her. She did not feel that either parent made her feel special, as they were too busy sorting out themselves and their relationships, but during her trip abroad, she had developed aspects of herself that compensated for this. Returning to the place where Jade had actually lived during her phase of infantile omnipotence, she recaptured a defensive omnipotence and inflation, which covered her feelings of enraged inferiority. With hindsight it was too difficult for Jade to stay in therapy and risk a transference relationship that might confirm her inner expectations. Jade linked being ordinary to being like her mother – weak, and full of impotent and yet unsafe rage – and these were feelings that she did not want to think about. The intrusive, desperate mother/baby part of herself captivated her, and threatened to overwhelm her, so to shut her up Jade engaged in increasingly angry and destructive activities.

Chapter 6

The psychodynamics of the psychotherapeutic process with patients who are harming themselves

Transference and countertransference issues

Working with transference is clearly the backbone of analytic practice, but there are different and changing perspectives on the importance of transference and countertransference in work with young people. The first psychoanalytic account of work with an adolescent girl is the celebrated and much cited study by Freud (1905) of his treatment with 'Dora'. Dora first came to Freud's consulting room when she was 16, and entered treatment two years later in 1900 with symptoms of hysteria, intervals of depression and thoughts of suicide. She linked her difficulties to inappropriate sexual advances made to her by a family friend, Herr K., a man whose wife was having an affair with Dora's father. Freud's insistent and somewhat dogmatic interpretations focused on Dora's repressed sexual interest in Herr K., her father and Frau K. After eleven weeks she suddenly broke off her treatment with bad feelings. Interestingly Freud describes her sudden ending as acting out and a form of self-injury – he felt she enacted the vengeance she felt for Herr K. on Freud (1905: 109).

This 'self-injury' by Dora helped Freud really understand the power and usefulness of transference as an analytic tool. He already understood that patients experienced inappropriate loving and hateful feelings in analysis based on their early infantile experiences; he now saw that transference was partly a resistance to the process of analytic work (Freud 1912). Later he wrote of transference as a re-enactment of an earlier relationship with someone significant; this meant that the patient endowed the analyst with meaning and expected them to behave accordingly, leaving no space for self-reflection – it was therefore a resistance to insight and change until it could be interpreted and relinquished (Freud 1917a).

A well-known feature of this case is Freud's recognition that he had not seen the strength of Dora's transference to him. He also did not acknowledge his own countertransference – his transference to Dora. This latter is a concept that we know has changed and developed over the years since Freud. At the time of Dora's treatment she was experiencing all the confusion, body changes and psychic conflict already discussed, and it would be these very feelings involving the adolescent state of mind that would have been reactivated in Freud.

Apparently at Dora's age, Freud too was preoccupied with confused longings. According to documentation (Gay 1988), he had a close, confiding friendship with another young man, Eduard Silberstein, and Freud confessed to an 'agreeable, wistful feeling' at his friend's absence and to his 'longing' to meet with him. He had also fallen for the sister of another school friend, a girl called Gisela Fluss. However, in his correspondence with Eduard, Freud dwelled on the charms of the girl's mother: 'Frau Fluss ... was the true target of his taciturn, fleeting adolescent passion' (Gay 1988: 23). Such feelings if not the memories of these long-ago adolescent passions – both homosexual and heterosexual, with a young woman and her mother – would probably have been reactivated in Freud and indeed may have unconsciously influenced his treatment of Dora.

Countertransference has a variety of meanings with a measure of diversity regarding the extension of the concept (cf. Gabbard 1995; Hinshelwood 1999). Generally it is viewed as including the whole of the psychotherapist's unconscious reactions to the patient, rather than limiting it to the unconscious processes evoked in the psychotherapist by the patient's transferences. Both kinds overlap, and, in both, the counter-transference is seen as a way of helping the psychotherapist understand the latent meaning behind the patient's communications, through monitoring their own mental associations while listening to the patient.

Countertransference is acknowledged to be especially intense and profound, and therefore more difficult to overcome, in work with young people (Haim 1974). This is partly because of the volatility in the patient and the strength of all the primitive and confused feelings that are present. In working with young people, both the re-emergence of one's own adolescent confusion and the patient's projected feelings are terribly disruptive and uncomfortable. Feelings such as stupidity, helplessness, humiliation and persecution reflect how the young person has felt and aspects of their processes of her internal object relations.

Anna Freud describes how an adolescent may change rapidly in mood or emotion, 'leaving the analyst little time and scope to marshal his forces and change his handling of the case according to the changing need' (1958: 261). This is one reason why the countertransference, and careful self-analysis of it, is especially important in all therapeutic work with young people. The other reason is that the reactivation of the therapist's own difficulties can lead to resistance in the therapist, which in turn can lead to a sense of stagnancy in the therapy. Heimann's advice is that the analyst has to be able to '*sustain* the feelings that are stirred up in him, as opposed to discharging them (as does the patient), in order to *subordinate* them to the analytic task'. She urges contemplation rather than action (1950: 82). Winnicott warned that one danger in working with adolescents is the awakening of the part of ourselves that has not had its adolescence. This may lead the psychotherapist to resent adolescents' 'phase of the doldrums and makes us want to find a solution for them' (Winnicott 1984: 155). In other words, psychotherapists who did not act out or risk take and had a relatively quiet adolescence might feel furious with patients who cause a lot of trouble, and throw away good opportunities.

In the work with patients who are harming themselves, the therapeutic task is to shift the intrapsychic conflict – previously held by attacking the body – to containment of the conflict through transference. This includes recognition of the dynamics of the encaptive conflict as it emerges in the dynamics between therapist and patient. This involves a shift towards fulfilment of the fantasy about the interpersonal relationship with the therapist, a movement from action and sensation to thought. The patient is searching for a relationship with the therapist that repeats and so confirms the patient's unconscious fantasy expectations of bondage to an avaricious and tyrannical object and the need to cut free. She is also searching for a new love object that might heal and gratify. The transference, both positive and negative, can become split, with one aspect displaced on to someone other than the therapist.

The following two brief clinical examples illustrate, first, the split transference, and second, transference to the total analytic situation. In the first example, Linda, discussed in Chapter 5, was referred for weekly psychotherapy sessions through the social services department. She had been cutting and had also taken an overdose. Initially Linda did not want to come, and felt forced to by her social worker. The transference was negative for the first few months, and Linda was reluctant to talk in the sessions, eventually voicing concerns that I might let her down and reject her. When we looked at this more carefully there were glimpses of the encaptive conflict. Linda showed her fear of being taken over by me, that I might be critical and denigrating, and that I would not like what I saw. At the same time she longed for a close, accepting relationship, so that if she became dependent she might have to stay, no matter how awful she felt. Over time it became clearer that how Linda saw herself, and expected others to see her, derived from her internalised experiences with her mother. This relationship seemed to have been difficult for as long as Linda could remember, with her mother openly critical and apparently preferring the boys in the family. Not surprisingly, Linda dressed in boys' clothing and eschewed anything remotely feminine. In the transference, she expected that I would be as critical and rejecting as she had experienced her mother to be.

The split transference was demonstrated through Linda's relationship with her young drama teacher, who seemed to offer a mutually, close and confiding relationship, inviting Linda to her house for tea one day after school, and telling her about her own problems. Linda felt excited by this relationship and imagined she might be in love with the teacher. This lasted for several months, and during that time Linda talked to me a great deal about the relationship. It seemed that she had formed a very positive transference, and as if she had achieved the longed-for fusion with an idealised mother. She felt she was in love, and contrasted the intimacy with this teacher to the rather formal structure of the psychotherapy with me. In the countertransference I became increasingly irritated with the situation, and was aware that I felt in competition for Linda's affections. Linda said she was cross that I wouldn't tell her about myself and invite her to my home. Linda's demands on the teacher increased over the summer holiday. She told me she visited the teacher's home almost every day, offering to do odd jobs such as mow the lawn or help decorate the house. The emergence of the rather possessive, overwhelming part of herself in this object relationship led to her experiencing rejection and feeling criticised when the teacher explained that she had to keep the distinction between teacher and pupil clearer. Linda then felt the teacher disliked her and the friendship ended. Linda became angry and upset about people who let her down. She was able to say that she was worried that the same might happen with me, and later made a link to times she remembered when she had felt she could be close to her mother, only for this closeness to abruptly end. It also became easier to talk about both the good and bad feelings that Linda felt in transference.

In the next example, Kathy, a 'tomboy' who loved all – but especially stray – animals, was referred following repeated hitting of her fists against walls. This had led to serious bruising and injury to her knuckles. She described her huge feelings of frustration and rage before the hitting. After the attacks, although bruised and bleeding, Kathy would feel calmer. In the transference Kathy felt uncertain about psychotherapy – she wanted to come to sessions, but was worried about talking about her feelings and becoming upset. She felt happier describing the animals she met and knew, and had an empathic link with those who had been neglected or abandoned.

Kathy had had no contact with her natural mother for over three years, and had ambivalent feelings about contact with her. She had recurring dreams about meeting her mother, and feared both the conflict and intimacy of such a meeting. Her anxiety developed into a transference to the entire analytic situation. On the way to sessions Kathy began to feel very anxious that her mother might suddenly appear and confront her. The fantasy of actual captivation by a tyrannical and overwhelming mother had emerged with terrifying force. This fear developed into panic attacks whenever she saw a white car near the building where we met. She thought that it might be her mother's new husband coming to get her. It was clear that the sessions evoked terribly difficult feelings in her, and all sorts of repressed feelings about her mother began to emerge through the transference. However, it seemed that aspects of the encaptive conflict had been displaced on to the fantasy mother who might appear outside the building, rather than be held by me in the consulting room. Kathy was able to talk about some of her confused and painful feelings. She was angry with me for messing her head up, and although she came to sessions she wished she did not have to. After some time, Kathy saw that, mixed up in all her anger towards her mother, there was also a longing to actually see her again and find out for herself what kind of person she was. In the end contact was made, but, after initial enthusiasm, Kathy became disillusioned by her mother and ended up feeling let down again by her, though this time she did not feel so afraid of her.

Young people can sometimes find transference interpretations embarrassing and overly intimate, while others welcome the relief of the recognition by the therapist of previously inexpressible feelings. The transference is always present, but the timing and necessity of inter-pretation is dependent on individual factors. The positive transference is recognised in the patient's welcome and love for the therapist's concern and interest in who they are rather than their cutting. The negative is recognised in the patient's hatred for the therapist's insistence on under-standing rather than condoning or condemning the acting out of their self-destruction. If the young woman can begin to understand her anger and hatred through the transference, then she may not need to direct it at her own body.

If the self-harming behaviour does not change as a response to insight, and remains as driven and dangerous despite verbalisation, there might develop a paranoid transference. In this situation the patient's hatred towards the therapist can lead to feelings of great anxiety, when the patient feels she can no longer keep safe from her own destructive wishes, and so the therapeutic relationship is liable to break down. At this point the self-harm could come to represent an identification with a sadistic therapist, and at the same time the body that is under attack stands for the therapist who is being punished for not making everything better. One solution would be to try to increase the intensity of the sessions, which would allow more opportunity to contain the encaptive conflict in the sessions rather than by cutting.

There has been much debate about the transference issue in work with young people. The central subject is how appropriate transference interpretations are for adolescent patients, given the revival of infantile attachments which the young person is trying to leave behind. However, more often than not the troubled adolescent is unable to reach a phase of successful detachment, and actual and/or emotional separation from the parents is part of the problem. My view is that the person of the psychotherapist can be used as a new experience alongside the patient's unconscious need to repeat earlier object relations, and that separation issues can be worked through in the transference. Influential here is the work of Anna Freud, who distinguishes the healthy part of the personality as the part that sees the therapist as a new object, while the transference is of use with the more disturbed aspects of the young patient's personality. She points out the difficulties inherent in such a double relationship and the need to move carefully between the two roles (Freud 1969: 38). This assumption that the transference leads to regressive dependence on the psychotherapist is taken up by the Laufers (1984, 1989) who argue that the ill adolescent who is unable to detach from the parental objects is experiencing a continued dependence. They feel that it is only through dependency on the analyst that there is an opportunity to manage, contain and reshape the conflicts which result from this dependency.

This brings me to situations where the patient is seriously at risk, and when the psychotherapist has to take over the caring function. This can be one characteristic of transference in work with patients who are repeatedly harming themselves. The danger of taking on this position is that the young woman, through her behaviour or acting out, may be using the psychotherapist to live out and gratify regressive fantasies rather than analyse them. However, what at times feels like an unconscious collusion can be a way through which the adolescent feels herself cared for, potentially leading to the recognition that she does not need to reject or attack her body. This dilemma may be illustrated by further material from my clinical practice.

Laura (discussed in Chapter 3) was referred for cutting herself and risk-taking behaviour involving cumulative taking of a variety of pills. These were not clear overdoses, for, as Laura described it, she wanted to see how far she could push her body and how weird she could make herself feel. Laura had been admitted for a short while to a residential unit, but had not co-operated with the family therapy treatment offered. She had found it too difficult to sit with her parents discussing what had happened in the family and how they all felt about it. She had specifically asked for psychotherapy because she said she wanted to understand why she was behaving the way she was. However, it did seem that part of her rationale for individual sessions was that whatever happened remained private and a secret from her parents. At one level the very arrangements for the treatment then replicated both her self-harming behaviour and the earlier abusive experiences. The difference was that I was now involved, and a witness to what Laura brought to the sessions.

In one sense therefore Laura was motivated to attend; she came to sessions and was anxious if for any reason she was late, but in other ways she was difficult in the therapeutic situation. She seemed to bring with her an aura of defensiveness. At her request I had no direct contact with her parents, who were not even to know if or when she came to sessions, although they had continuing contact with the residential unit. In the early sessions she was frequently silent, ignoring my interpretations or reflections. Towards the end of the sessions she would sometimes finally say in a stilted manner that she had nothing to say, and saw no point in coming as she did not see how talking could possibly change anything or make her feel differently. She did not want to tell me anything about her family or her life at college, but her continuing symptoms revealed the strength of her rage and despair. It seemed that she was inextricably bound to a punishing inner object, possibly linked to the internalisation of the processes derived from the dynamics of the sexual abuse she had experienced over many years.

I did my best to tolerate her omnipotence and feelings of self-sufficiency and control, but this was difficult because of the powerful projections involved. In the transference she needed to have my complete attention and concentration. She would scrutinise my face from her position in the chair opposite to me, and when I spoke she listened to the sound of my voice for any deviation of tone or hint of rejection towards her from me. If my attention wavered, I became the rejecting, uninterested mother who put other concerns before her daughter. Despite Laura's longing to be understood, revealed in her conscious statement that she wanted to understand herself and her regular attendance, any hint of the realisation of this longing felt dangerous and led to attacks on me in the transference.

As Laura started to trust me she talked a little more, and her need to be understood and accepted emerged more clearly. Laura became frightened by the strength of her longings, and her self-harming behaviour increased. She would tell me of certain incidents, and the gruesome descriptions of harming created a distance between us. This now seemed to be all that there was to speak about, and so a more meaningful relationship between us was avoided. There was a danger that I could become involved in a false alignment or even friendship with this excited, destructive part of herself. It seemed as if the cutting represented a form of 'splitting', in that she wanted to describe the injury and her fascination with it, but not the feelings associated with why she had to do this. If I suggested how she might be feeling, Laura dismissed this with derision, and I frequently found it difficult to find ways of making a connection with her. Over time I felt increasingly persecuted by her sharp responses, and tended to tone down and limit my interpretations and contributions. In the countertransference I had a flavour of her encaptive psychic conflict. I felt trapped by what felt like her relentless and regular attendance, controlled by her critical, ironical and derisive responses to my interpretations of what she said, and, perversely, enthralled by her descriptions of injuries.

I would like to focus on one specific dilemma in the transference and countertransference with Laura, and what this meant. This was when I felt the need to directly take on the caring function. As her defensive stance became less powerful, Laura slowly began to realise her emotional vulnerability. This was demonstrated when she felt increasingly anxious about any breaks or interruptions in the therapy. She would firmly dismiss my thoughts about her feelings to do with the breaks, but in the sessions preceding one long summer break she told me of even more incidents of cutting and how she was gathering different sorts of pills for experimentation. In my countertransference I was filled with a sense of helplessness, and felt worried and stressed by her threats. None of my interpretations about Laura feeling let down and left on her own with the interruption to the sessions seemed to relieve the general unease and anxious atmosphere.

In the final session before my holiday, Laura, unusually, was five minutes late and remained silent for the first part of the session. Her face showed resentment and misery, and she responded to my reflections with shrugs and grimaces. Fuelled by frustration and anxiety, I eventually commented that I could see that it all felt difficult, but that I couldn't help her if she didn't tell me what the matter was. Laura then acknowledged that something had happened at home earlier that day, and by deduction I gathered that she and her mother had quarrelled after her mother had found blood on Laura's duvet. She added how stupid her mother was: it was obvious to anyone that the way the blood had marked the duvet was not how it was if one had cut oneself in the ordinary way. Laura added that she had to carry everything important and necessary for her cutting and pill taking around with her in a bag in case her mother found out anything more; she was always poking about in Laura's room.

In the negative transference I could see Laura felt that I was always intruding inside her, trying to find things out, but at the same time there was a positive transference to a mother who did show concern, and might help to contain these powerful and destructive impulses. She told me that she was hurting herself and drawing blood, though she added that she did not want to say how she was doing it, and this I accepted. This time I did not feel any interest at all in what Laura was actually doing to herself. I felt I did not want to know, although I could see that Laura was trying to tantalise me about the actual method of injury. She also told me that when she left the session she would be looking for other ways to cause herself pain. She thought she might get a tattoo done wherever it would hurt most – she mused about which part of her skin that would be, her mother would disapprove and it would cause Laura physical pain, which was what she said she wanted. All further interpretations to do with the feelings about separation were heard but shrugged away, and I felt my concern increase.

Towards the end of the session Laura, sounding more excited, said that she could not decide whether to tell me how much I annoyed her. I said that I thought she was telling me just that, and how confused the angry and needy parts of her made her feel. Laura said that it was not just this week, it was every week: I just sat there, all I was doing was my job and then that was that. I replied that perhaps she was wondering whether I thought about her when I was not just doing my job, especially over a break. Her response was to shrug and shake her head. After a silence I suggested she might have fantasies about who else I might be with or thinking about. Perhaps it felt as if I just dropped her and was not there for her when she was left feeling so bad. Laura remained silent and glared at me. She then repeated about it just being a job, and I commented that she sometimes needed to think that I might be like a robot and not have feelings about her, especially when she felt so cross with me and so mixed up about the break. Laura replied that she did not care, she was not listening to me. She just could not decide where to have the tattoo done. I suggested that she might worry about how I felt about her, especially after telling me how annoyed she felt.

After the session I was left feeling concerned both about her capacity to hurt and punish herself, and her resistance to understanding all the mixed-up emotions. I realised that I too felt angry with her – leaving me filled with these worries before my holiday. A further misgiving was that she had few friends, and she had rejected all plans to go away over the summer. This was a situation where I felt I needed support and consultation. Following discussion in a supervision session, I decided to set up a safety net both for Laura and indirectly myself, by involving the doctor, the residential unit she had stayed in and the family therapist who was still working with Laura's parents. Laura already knew that other colleagues were covering at the clinic, but I wrote to her explaining that these additional support systems were in place if everything felt too much. I realised that in the transference I was taking on the caring function and so providing Laura with some gratification, but in my countertransference I needed to feel some security and relief from my anxiety.

It was a relief to meet with her after the summer, and to find that she had survived and barely harmed herself. In her rather dismissive manner she told me that she had ended up having a really good summer, and had in the end gone away to stay with some cousins where there had been lots of partying and drinking. In hindsight it turned out to be me who was left with all the anxiety about the break – Laura did not bother to get the tattoo done. Did I act out, collude and so gratify Laura through my concern, which led to setting up a care plan for the summer holiday? Well, yes, I now think that I did, in that I had become overly caught up with the projected fear of her actual destructive impulses, rather than holding on to what I knew from my experience in the transference. I was left stuck with this introjected aspect and weighed down by the anxiety that fuelled her destructive behaviour. None the less, remembering the feelings and the worry that I brought to that supervision session, I think I would probably do the same again given the circumstances. By the time we finished working together, Laura had stopped cutting and had reduced her experimentation with pills. She was more interested in talking about and having a social life with her friends.

Transference and countertransference can be intensely and profoundly experienced by both therapist and patient. The feelings that are evoked in the transference with patients who are harming themselves can often cause discomfort and anxiety, and provoke a demand that the therapist relate or behave in a way that eases this tension. Young women who are harming themselves often want the therapist to understand and thereby condone the attacks being made on the body. They are looking for support in the solution they have found for the unbearable psychic conflict. Under such strong pressure the psychotherapist has to maintain the boundaries and hold the responsibility for trying to understand the meanings behind the action, so that the anxiety is experienced and the reasons for it eventually understood well enough by the patient. The task is to understand that what has appeared irreconcilable can eventually be accepted and managed. The co-existence of two sets of feelings of both love and hate and the achievement of a position of ambivalence is possible. The pain and gain from insight is acquired through the knowledge of the gradual acquaintance with oneself.

Projection and projective identification

Projection can be seen as a defence based on repression of an unacceptable intrapsychic experience. This is what is projected on to the therapist. The patient does not want to know about the feeling, and so distances herself from it. This was my experience in the earlier account of working with Laura. Splitting, not repression, is seen as a central part of the process of projective identification which involves the projection of intolerable (rather than unacceptable) aspects of an intrapsychic experience into the therapist. Unconsciously the patient maintains empathy with what is projected, and attempts to control the object as part of the defence by inducing in the object what is projected. In Bion's (1962) model of the container, the analyst contains the intolerable feelings of anxiety, fear and rage which the patient puts into the object. As a consequence of 'maternal reverie' – a process of making sense of what is happening – these awful feelings are returned to the patient as assimilable interpretations.

As was seen in the work with Laura, the therapist can increasingly become the focus for many of the projections, especially the projection of hopelessness and destructiveness. The cumulative effect of containing projections of sadism and destruction can leave the therapist with depleted resources. If the process of introjection and projection breaks down between the therapist and patient, the therapist can become stuck with a damaged introjected part of the patient, and a form of stalemate is reached, with no apparent movement possible in the treatment. One of the effects of this is an experience of contamination. The therapist contains but cannot return the feelings to the patient. This will be especially so if the patients themselves lack the capacity to mentally represent, as I discussed in Chapter 5. The danger is then that the psychotherapist becomes overwhelmed by the patient's experiences – this is certainly the situation if the contamination includes unprocessed aspects of the encaptive conflict. This state will be exacerbated if the psychotherapist is very busy with too many similar patients, so allowing insufficient time to identify and reflect on the different countertransference experiences. Regular exposure to such powerful projective processes can lead to the belief that the therapist is no good, and has nothing helpful to say. Powerful projections can also be experienced somatically as particular body pains or nausea either during or after the session. In such circumstances the weight of the destructive impulses is being carried by the therapist. However, if insufficient care is taken to deal with these issues these aspects can prove destructive for the psychotherapist, who may feel very stressed and worn out by the work.

Little warns us about the effect of projection and projective identi-fication. She writes about the powerful stimulus of what she describes as 'the extensively disintegrated personality [which] touches on the most deeply repressed and carefully defended danger spots in the analyst, and correspondingly the most primitive (and incidentally least effective) of his defense mechanisms are called into play' (1986: 42). In other words, the disturbing patient will unerringly find our most vulnerable parts, sometimes leaving us weakened in our response. These processes have to be understood, acknowledged and managed in the light of the patient's transferences. Obviously regular and sufficient supervision of the work with people who self-harm is essential. A good-enough support matrix needs to be maintained for all those involved in this sort of work, which includes thinking about case management alongside the dynamics of the work.

With some young women who are cutting there seems at times an emotional flatness and an inhibition of thinking. As has been discussed, the therapist can only too easily become identified with this deadening anti-thinking aspect. With such patients, who have serious character pathology and unconsciously escape their intolerable intrapsychic experiences by projective identification, it may be relatively easy to pick up the projective identification, but more difficult to interpret because of the patient's resistance and dread of what had to be projected in the first place. With other patients who are able to talk about their experiences projective identification tends to be more subtle, but if the psychotherapist remains unrestricted – in other words, free to fantasise and think – it can be handled through interpretation. The following example explores in some depth the projective processes with a patient who was relatively mature and able to talk about her experiences. Her main defence was repression, not splitting, and when projective identification occurred it was subtle, and I was given space to fantasise and think about what she was saying.

Diana (who was discussed in Chapter 4) was referred aged 19 for weight loss, cutting and hitting herself, and was taken on for weekly psychotherapy for a year. Initially in the transference I sometimes represented an available and listening mother, and she would leave me feeling concerned and responsible for her well-being. At times this also felt like a countertransference response and gave me insight into her own feelings of concern and responsibility as a child for her parents, especially towards her mother. Early on Diana brought a dream. In it a huge fat woman was fighting and beating Diana up; the blows really hurt and she felt that her body hurt all over. As she glanced over she could see her parents watching from the side. While they both looked anxious they did not really seem to see or hear what was going on, and did nothing to help. This dream enabled Diana to gain a sense of what she was physically doing to herself, and to begin to allow some thoughts that perhaps her parents were not as perfect as she initially insisted. The dream helped me understand my countertransference experiences, where I felt anxious about the ways that she hurt herself and yet at the same time observant and detached from feelings. Furthermore it gave a glimpse of the encaptive conflict – an intrapsychic object relationship involving a suffocating, avaricious, fat part of Diana involved in a sadistic attack on a more vulnerable, small, victim part of herself.

As the weeks passed, Diana was able to talk about herself and her difficult feelings of envy and hostility towards another sibling, and her perception of this sibling's better relationship with their parents. Diana began to talk about her need to control the family and to a lesser extent myself in the sessions. She insisted that she knew that I was on her side, unlike her mother and the consultant psychiatrist involved in monitoring her weight and self-injury. In the countertransference I felt this control whenever Diana commented on my responses or any sign that led her to suppose that I was irritated or disinterested in her. In this way I began to experience this rather suffocating, all-encompassing aspect of some of the processes belonging to her internal world.

As the transference deepened, Diana became more disturbed whenever there were holiday breaks. Sometimes she felt let down and abandoned. Initially she denied feelings of dependency and involvement in the therapy, but gradually spoke about her need to seek revenge on me by cutting herself. The cutting was one of the reasons she was being seen by me. However, she said it would hurt and upset me if she went on cutting herself, even though she was coming to therapy. The cutting represented an attack on me as associated with the overwhelming and sadistic part of herself. It seemed that in her mind we were undifferentiated; the cutting both destructively fused us together and demonstrated another part of her that wanted to cut and separate us. Sometimes Diana was able to express her anger in the sessions and attack the therapy and myself. Initially this increased her cutting, but as she realised that we might both survive her outbursts, and that the therapy would continue whether or not she cut herself, the cutting gradually abated.

In a session around the Easter break she was openly angry and upset yet found it hard to know why she felt so terrible. In the counter-transference I felt like giving up on her – a projection that reflected her feelings that everyone, including myself, had had enough of her. She was projecting her anxiety about separation and abandonment, as well as her own feelings of giving up on herself. I suggested that Diana might be feeling anxious about the interruption to our sessions. Diana's response was to speak of her need to leave home, where she felt excluded and rejected. She said that with me she felt pushed out and left to get on with it at the end of each session, and especially when there was a holiday.

In another session she was full of derision about psychotherapy and the sort of people who needed it. She spoke of being in the waiting room before the session with other people. She described one as a fat, selfish and self-absorbed young child who made continual demands of an exhausted mother – she presumed that this child was also waiting for a therapy session. Diana then cynically asked me to 'analyse' her, and tell her what she was thinking. I now think the perceived scene in the waiting room was partly how she experienced her inner object relationship – the fat, selfish, overwhelming aspect of herself deeply dependent on an exhausted, more mothering/victim part of herself. She derided her vulnerability and her need to be psychically fed and attended to by me in the transference. The empty, unfilled places inside her terrified her, and her increasing dependency on me evoked fears of further enslavement. She was anxious also about exhausting me by her demands. She was able to see that this connected with her anxiety when much younger about her mother's capacity to contain and meet her needs. Despite responding to my interpretations, Diana minimised and denigrated her need of me by commenting that I had to see her because I was paid to, and this left her feeling less guilty. Following sessions when she was so dismissive of me (indeed her manner could be described as cutting), she became anxious about my welfare and survival. I was relieved by her ability to think about her strong feelings, and the conscious recognition of the strength of them.

As her psychic conflict grew clearer it became easier for Diana to talk about her family and about separating from them. She was also preoccupied with our relationship – was I really interested in her and wanting to see her, or just putting it on because I was being paid to do so? If I was just doing my job, she wondered how many other girls I saw. I think this revealed both Diana's longing for fusion – that I really wanted her and only her – and her concomitant fear of being either engulfed by me or abandoned because of all the others who displaced her. In my countertransference response it was possible for me to maintain empathy with her central subjective experience, and our relationship was relatively free of more primitive defences, especially of strong projective identification. She had repressed many feelings and she projected aspects of her intrapsychic experiences on to family members and on to myself as psychotherapist. By the end of the year's therapy Diana was able to leave home to do the courses that she wanted.

The next, longer, example I give is of work with Anne, who has been discussed before in the book. For some patients, especially those who are more seriously disturbed, projective identification tends to dominate the treatment. While projective identification is seen as a primitive defensive operation, the process can open a way to dialogue and lead to understanding, but this undoubtedly depends on the capacity of the psychotherapist to manage and contain the patient's projections. The containing function, according to Rosenfeld (1987), requires a great deal more than passivity – rather the analyst has to be prepared to enter an intense relationship and retain his or her function of putting experiences into words. The patient usually requires a great deal of active thinking from the psychotherapist because she herself lacks the capacity for doing so. 'The analyst has to bring together the diffuse, confused or split-up aspects of the patient's pre-thought processes in his own mind so that they gradually make sense and have meaning' (1987: 160).

Some of the potential difficulties and dangers of this process are well understood, including the possibility of the breakdown of verbal communication between patient and psychotherapist which may lead to misunderstanding and misinterpretation by the patient. This can be connected to the patient's incapacity for abstract thinking, as discussed earlier, when words and their meanings may be experienced by the patient as concrete, non-symbolic objects. In some situations the disturbed patient may find interpretations critical and frightening, and she may use projective identification as a way of denying painful feelings.

Anne was seen intensively over four years. She had had a disrupted and damaging early childhood with a drug-addicted mother and several periods in foster homes. Following a move to live with her father she was sexually abused by another relative. From early adolescence Anne began to hurt her body, and after several stays in hospital she went to an adolescent unit. She found psychotherapy immensely difficult, but said that she wanted to keep coming to sessions. She had no other commitments, so the structure of our regular sessions provided some sort of framework for her life. In the first months she sat stiffly, looking away from me. She rarely spoke, responding with 'I don't know' to my attempts at reflective commentary or interpretations about what I thought might be going on. She was cutting regularly and incisively, leaving deep scars that formed into large, discoloured lumps on her arms and thighs. At that time in the countertransference I experienced emotions that included strong feelings of despair, hopelessness and inertia. As Anne became more used to our meetings she found it slightly easier to speak about external events. On some occasions when I suggested what she might be feeling, she responded to the experienced intrusion with an angry outburst about the futility of speaking about pain. I felt devalued and dejected in the sessions, and would remember all the other apparently failed therapeutic attempts with Anne that had taken place over the years.

About six months into the work Anne brought in poems that she had written for me to read. Despite this, every session felt fragile and tentative, and it began to become clearer to me that she felt overwhelmed both by her own experiences and any attempts by me to understand them. These projections meant that I would often struggle to find an appropriate word, feeling ill at ease, often doubting my own thoughts and experience. My words seemed to hang hollowly and foolishly in the air somewhere between us. Usually they were not even picked up by Anne, and appeared to fade away long before reaching her. Away from the sessions, it struck me that I was feeling exactly as she did about the futility of speaking and the impossibility of words as a way of conveying feelings. At an unconscious level Anne needed to protect something very small and weak within herself from being extinguished. Therefore she needed to get rid of any disturbing thoughts and feelings. When terrible things had happened or happened in the present, Anne would shrug and say that she had no feelings about any of it. I had to learn to accept this attitude and recognise the cutting as one of the ways she had found of coping. Anne warned me 'don't try to stop me cutting – I'll die if I can't cut'. Anne's and my dilemma seemed encapsulated by this statement.

I would like to describe part of a session two and a half years into the treatment, and then part of the following session. Anne arrived about ten minutes late, and was as usual dressed all in black, and looking very pale. Her arms and legs were covered in layers of clothing. She sat silently and stiffly in front of me. After a few moments of silence I asked about her evening out with her girl-friend – an unusual activity for Anne. She gave me some details and then explained that she had had to borrow money from her stepmother to cover it, she had just received her benefit, and she would have to pay the money back straight away, leaving her with virtually nothing. Then she added 'and I've got the journey to the hospital to pay for and my friend's wedding all in the same fortnight'.

This evoked in me difficult feelings about deprivation and guilt, and my response was to suggest that while I was aware that she always felt she had to pay money back straight away, perhaps it could wait this time. My guilt led me to feel that Anne was being very obstinate and prim when she replied in a stubborn way, 'I don't like owing people money'. I reminded her that she could get the money back for the trip to the hospital, where she was to have some of the deep scars operated on. Anne said that she would not know how to get the money, she hadn't been able to ask her friend to go with her to the hospital because it was only two days before the friend's wedding. Anyway, she was sure it was only a local anaesthetic and so she would go on her own.

Again I felt flooded with an awareness of abandoning her, and felt in touch with her desperate sense of having to manage everything on her own. I also felt cross with her sustained passivity, and realised as I had often done how terribly angry Anne was – even though she always denied it. I decided to say something about her feelings about managing alone, and she responded with 'I don't mind' and 'he's only doing two of the cuts'. In the countertransference I then felt very sad, and silence fell.

Unexpectedly Anne broke the silence by asking whether I had seen a television programme called *An Inspector Calls*. She then described how there was a really filthy house, and the inspectors from the council had had to go and deal with it. She added 'it's just that it was just like my mum's house. You see people don't believe me when I tell them how awful it was, and it was like the one on television. People always think I'm exaggerating.' She then went on to speak, with some encouragement from me, about the awfulness of her mum's house, and what she remembered about it. Eventually the house had been redecorated and carpeted, but before then it was a mess. The worst thing for her was the brown in the sink and toilet, it was like that in the house in the film – even if you cleaned it it would not come off, and anyway, she added, there were never any cleaning materials. Anne went on to describe how there had been an infestation in all the junk in the garden, with flies everywhere. She said 'that's what I like about my flat, because it's new and I'm on the first floor. I've never had any spiders and if I keep my windows shut there are no flies. . . . I feel phobic about that.'

I reflected back her need to keep all the bad things out, and how important it was for her to be different from her mother. This prompted her to give more descriptions of her mother's house about mould and decay, adding that she did not understand how people could be like that and not bother. This session was the most animated that we had over the entire four years, but was followed by two cancelled sessions – one for the hospital appointment and one missed session with no reason given.

The session ended before I could sort out my thoughts – there had not been space for me to fantasise or think, and I realised later that I had not fully understood the implications of the internal inspector calling. For Anne it was imperative that she make herself safe from degradation and contamination, as represented by her external and internal mother, by being utterly whiter than white. The deprivation and guilt that I had felt was part of the projection of an intolerable aspect of her own intrapsychic experience. In her mind the stains would never go, and there were no means available to remove them. The captivation by an overwhelming, abusive part of herself remained, no matter how much she tried to clean and cut it out. My interpretation about managing alone went against her current purging and cleansing of herself, and in that sense was irrelevant. In her description of the dirty house Anne saw herself as beyond redemption. The important aspect was to let nothing more in, and in that sense all words/interpretations felt persecutory and contaminating. She was looking for an ally in her attempts to manage overwhelming guilt and despair resulting from the encaptive conflict. Her hope might be for an inspector who could redeem an impossible situation, but like her parents I was a failure. My failure to have seen the programme for myself, and my unsatisfactory responses in the session, seemed to have confirmed her sense of being the only one who knew how dreadful it all was, both inside and outside. In her perception I did not notice how hard it was for her to keep part of herself untainted.

When we met again Anne was silent and withdrawn, and barely looked at me. I commented on the long gap that we had had, but she said she could not remember that far back. With some encouragement she talked a little about the hospital appointment, but then silence fell. I linked her reluctance to speak with the missed sessions, and at this Anne became angry and retorted 'oh just ignore me'. I commented that perhaps it seemed as if I had ignored her over the gap – perhaps it felt as if I had let her down in some way. She shook her head in an angry dismissive way, as if I was the stupidest person in the world, and said 'it's nothing to do with that'. I felt irritated and dismissed. When I suggested that it might be to do with something else, she told me that she didn't feel well, she had pains in her stomach and felt very tired. When I wondered whether it was linked to her injuring herself, Anne became furious, said 'no' and began to cry.

I tried another interpretation to do with her worries about what was going on inside her body, which I later felt was more to relieve my own anxiety about her health and the session as a whole, and again she became angry, shook her head and said 'no'. I said that she was angry when I tried to make sense of what she was feeling and I did not seem able to get it right, and she responded that she did not know why she was crying, adding 'and you always have to find a reason for everything'. Anne then became silent and withdrawn, and did not respond until the end of the session when she commented on leaving, 'don't take what I say personally'. In this last part of the session I was left feeling rather squashed and almost completely hopeless. However, I did take some heart from her last remark, in that I saw a glimmer of relating to me both in the sense of her possible realisation that she had squashed me, and a recognition of myself as outside the transference.

I did realise that my comments about the missed sessions emerged like a reproach, and presumably confirmed her feelings of being under attack. I think that for Anne the missed sessions did not matter in themselves, but were possibly a way of maintaining a space free of what felt like a terrible tainting. At a concrete level, I think she saw my words as the unclean insects, spoken about in the earlier session, that might get inside her and contaminate her or her flat. This purity had to be maintained at all costs. She needed the time away from me. When I asked relentless questions about her physical health I became increasingly identified with the intrusive and abusive part of herself that I seemed unable to break free from. I seemed caught in a compulsion to continue my attacking despite her response.

At the time I had felt as if I had a sense of her earlier experience as an anxious child trying to help and make sense of her sick mother and her symptoms. However, I connected afterwards with the realisation that for Anne, both being sick and the cutting were ways of keeping things clean inside her; this was a form of purging of a place where stains and degradation could not reach. In her inner world the cutting also served to cut out an identity separate from the overwhelming, contaminating mother who made everything dirty and brown. Safety lay in a sterile, closed place where no one could get in. This early inner object relationship was compounded by the later sexual abuse. The internalised relationship resulting from the trauma kept Anne in bondage to a sadistic and tyrannical master/mother. The cutting represented the marks of these fused relationships and the attempts to cut loose.

Much later I understood this as projective identification of the encaptive conflict. As in the session extract it is possible to see the projection of an intolerable aspect of herself – the desperate child, the production of the corresponding internal attitude in myself, the subtle control over me by her withdrawn silence and then her rather denigrating remark about always finding a reason, which seemed to keep me in this projected aspect of herself. Her final remark as she left was partly, I think, a fear of the power of her own anger and hatred towards me in this session, in that she was at that moment, when I felt so hopeless and dejected, anxious not to destroy me as she felt her mother and her abuser had destroyed her. It was an attempt to preserve me as well as herself from the contaminating world. At another level, as already mentioned above, it may also have been her concern, and her sense of needing to see me as separate from what was going on. One difficulty in working with my countertransference with Anne was that at times the projective identification was so powerful that it was hard to maintain an inner space and freedom to deal with what was happening. There was little space for clarifying and understanding the countertransference reactions before attempting new strategies for interpretation of the transference. The working through seemed to happen outside the session time, and only in the session if I deliberately 'cut myself off' and dissociated from the situation as one way of gaining some space.

Four years' intensive work with this patient was difficult to evaluate. Clearly I had kept her out of institutions and indeed kept her alive over this period, and this could be seen as a justification of my work from the perspective of the rationale of the clinic. She had stopped cutting but still suffered from bouts of bulimia. She had also been given a relationship which she would not have experienced before in her life. However, both my supervisor and myself were aware that this was probably not enough. Doubtless her ingrained vulnerability will affect her future life experiences.

The psychotherapist as a 'new' object and a 'real' person

Certain aspects of the work are outside the psychodynamics of transference and projection, but exist alongside them and are affected by them. Together with the emergence of the patient's psychic conflict in the transference relationship, there is, especially when working with young people, an ongoing interest in new experiences. The psychotherapist is a new object and a real person who might be able to offer new perspectives and model different ways of responding to events and feelings. Wilson (1991) usefully writes of the particular responsibilities and characteristics of working with young people. He reminds us of the need to remain respectful of the adolescent state of mind, and the mass of contradictions that exist at the centre of that state. In turn the psychotherapist's position has to be contradictory: flexible and yet firm and reliable; active, sometimes directive, and yet listening and observing. There has to be some partial inversion of what both stand for in that the young person, by dint of her disturbance, agrees to come for psychotherapy and thereby compromises her independence. The psychotherapist in turn agrees to be flexible and forgoes something of his adult discipline. Wilson writes about the importance of what sort of person the psychotherapist is, and what he or she brings to the situation. He suggests that appropriate characteristics include a high degree of self-awareness; personal authority and integrity; access to a reasonably coherent, conceptual framework; and the capacity and readiness to be receptive (1991: 467).

Implicit in this reminder are the interpersonal influences, and the subjectivity of the psychotherapist. Acceptance of such subjectivity implies the particular, individual, personal responses, conscious and unconscious, that psychotherapists have to their patients. This is different from the countertransference focus on what patients do to psychotherapists; rather it is about the influence that patients have on psychotherapists, and how we as people are affected and altered by this experience. Certainly working with young people can always challenge, surprise and change us, however difficult and upsetting that may feel, while their self-absorption may preclude any real recognition of the other person and their autonomy.

The work with the young women described in this chapter necessitated objectivity as part of my subjectivity. A danger when working with people who harm themselves is that of empathic immersion leading to implicit collusion. This is the aspect discussed in the work with Laura in terms of a false alignment or making friends with the destructive part of the patient.

Seeing the world from the patient's perspective, with the repeated cutting as a valid way of expressing conflict, can only be a temporary position for the psychotherapist. There needs to be dissent, and recognition of the psychotherapist's different reality, so that the patient has a sense of how separate subjects respond to his or her objectification of them.

Part of the process of working with patients who are bound to such destructive processes primarily derived from object relations is the gradual realisation that the therapist is an object external to the thinking mind of the patient. Again the clinical work with Laura described above serves as an example of this. While I needed to attune myself to her predicament and understand the function of her self-harm, there came a point when I needed to represent my separate opinion on the dangers of her risk-taking behaviour, and find ways of opposing her intrapsychic sadism and aggression. The aggression could become interpsychic, and be spoken about between us once Laura recognised my opposing response. As a worker in an agency I carried responsibility for her treatment and well-being on behalf of the agency as well as in my role as psychotherapist. This demanded an additional and external objectification, alongside my empathic attempts to understand her inner world and my subjective perspective on that.

Chapter 7

Speculations on historical, cultural and social aspects

'By his wounds you have been healed.'

(1 Peter 2:25)

This chapter moves away from the personal psyche and the confines of the consulting room, and out into a wider perspective. Although the understanding of the specific meaning of self-harm for any individual has to be seen as the central concern, there is a case for positioning the behaviour in its social, cultural and historical context, as an added dimension and further contribution to understanding its meaning. The purpose of this chapter is partly to show that cutting and mutilating the body can be seen as a well-established part of our cultural heritage, alongside its more pathological and subjectively painful contemporary manifestation. The second purpose is to introduce speculation and discussion on another level of meaning which might illuminate self-harming behaviour. After all, it is striking that culturally sanctioned self-harming behaviours are viewed, and understood, as ways in which people have sought meaning, a sense of belonging, or as part of a purification and healing process, over many centuries. People have chosen to suffer in the belief that their behaviour might be beneficial to themselves and might also serve the society in which they live. Intriguingly such experiences are not defined as pathological, but rather accepted as part of the culture and of the social or historical framework.

Are there therefore implications for how we might think about self-harm in the twenty-first century? Is it always going to be self-destructive? Are there possible echoes of any of these earlier aspects in the contemporary near-epidemic prevalence of self-harm? Generally there are three main ways in which sanctioned self-harming behaviour has been or is justified and so given meaning: one way is the path of religious salvation; a second is the promotion of health and healing; a third is that it is part of the necessary maintenance of the social system. Is it at all possible that some of the aspects of contemporary self-harming behaviour have their roots in these profound human experiences of salvation, healing and seeking order? If so they are undoubtedly distorted variations of these experiences. One variation that could be suggested is that there is some sense in which cutting can be seen as a misguided, and ultimately unsuccessful, variation of a long-forgotten initiation rite. These questions and speculations are explored further throughout the chapter.

While the practice of doing things to the surface of the body goes back to the very earliest of societies, and is present throughout history, both the meaning and attitude to bodily surfaces and what is done to them have to be understood within specific cultural contexts. It is these different meanings that are briefly explored using some of the literature from anthropology, archaeology, religion, history and contemporary socially accepted practices. Obviously this can only be a partial and clearly selective overview which is approached and interpreted from an analytic and psychotherapeutic perspective located outside the particular academic disciplines involved. However, what I think this literature review ultimately does demonstrate, above all else, is human variability and complexity, alongside the capacity for social practices to change and re-emerge with different values attached to them. In that sense no knowledge, including analytic understanding, can be seen as complete or particular to itself.

Anthropological and archaeological findings

Ritual and magic were formerly part of everyday life, but in our rational, deductive contemporary culture they are usually associated with superstition, sensationalism and pathology. Beliefs in certain practices must have led to an immense amount of activity in many societies which is now lost, but traces of these can be found both in anthropological accounts and archaeological records. Among the anthropological accounts the details of different initiation ceremonies marking the transition from childhood to adulthood seem to have the greatest connection to some of the characteristics of self-harm discussed in this book. One difference is that in most of the puberty rites described in the literature, the injuries were inflicted by another person. Yet to a certain extent such behaviour can now be seen as a form of self-harming because the initiate 'actively' co-operated, or had to co-operate, as they were under inescapable parental and societal pressure to do so. In this sense the injured person gained some sort of gratification – if only in the sense of social approval – from the painful ritual. In these cultural contexts the painful attacks on the body were being made for the social 'good', and in that sense society and 'self' appear to be interchangeable. This of course is very different in our contemporary culture, where the idea of society is more nebulous, and the concept of 'self' and the primacy of the needs of the individual are very much to the fore.

The purpose of initiation is to bring about a clear change in the religious and social status of the person. In adolescence, a time of transition, this is about gaining the right to be admitted to the adult world. In general the traditions appear usually to be for the young person to undergo a series of ordeals, implying a ritual death (the death of childhood) followed by resurrection or regeneration into adulthood and adult knowledge. 'The puberty initiation represents above all the revelation of the sacred' (Eliade 1995: 3), and it also implies the revelation of sexuality. In most cases the different rites described by Eliade (1995) begin with the sometimes violent separation of the child from the mother symbolising the death of childhood and ignorance. They almost all involve some sort of marking or modification of the body – this is often circumcision and injury to the genitals of both boys and girls. The cutting and injury would have been preceded and followed by various other ordeals, including fasting, and much ceremony and celebration in the social grouping. Through the rites the entire community is also regenerated and the social or tribal grouping is confirmed. The effects of such rites confirmed the young person's place in the society. It served to place the sexual life of the girl under social control, and detached the boy from his mother, so allowing his entry into the male community.

In describing initiation rituals of girls Eliade (1995) comments on how these are less dramatic than those for boys who inevitably have the greater show and ceremony, and tend to be in a group. In contrast, girls begin their initiation individually with the onset of menstruation and it is a time of segregation and isolation often in darkness, and more often than not on their own. Some of the rituals described by Menninger (1935) focus on the use of knives to cut the body of the initiate girls and boys. A recent research study on male initiation among the Yiwara of central Australia demonstrated how each stage of the initiation process was marked by its own particular form of mutilation, the pain apparently serving as a reminder of the significance of the events (Mitchell and Plug 1997). Unlike contemporary self-harm with its connotations of defeat, these attacks on the body are made with awareness, handed down from one generation to another. The rituals are publicly accepted, witnessed and celebrated, and the social meaning and individual implications are of transformation and ownership of the self.

Both Eliade and Menninger demonstrate their awareness of and insight into the unconscious factors connected with initiation rites. These are not just quaint customs, but rituals imbued with meaning. For example, Menninger (1935) suggests various reasons for cutting the genitals and other parts of the body. He views the injuries described in puberty rites as serving as ways of overcoming the incest taboo and the Oedipus complex, and therefore as part of the negotiation of moving into adult status. One reason is that the initiation rite serves as a way for parents to contain their hostility towards the adolescent for separating from their authority. Another is that it acts as a punishment for incestuous longings. A third reason is that it functions as a way of suppressing the adolescent's aggressive and sexual feelings. The rites also suggest atonement for future actions, and the price to be paid for acceptance into adulthood. Another suggestion is that the cutting of the genitals provides a symbolic castration – a part for the whole – and so acts as a propitiatory action. Menninger (1935: 438) also quotes Money-Kyrle's analysis of rituals that involve a part of the cut flesh, such as the foreskin, or a forcibly extracted tooth, being hidden in a tree; this he thinks serves to relive the neurotic fear of death.

If, as Eliade (1995) suggests, initiation is a universal rite that surfaces and influences life whenever there is a spirit of beginning or the weight of an end, then it will continue to emerge but in different guises. Rap bands, street gangs, prisons, cults, training organisations, military institutions and so on all contain initiatory rites and symbols. One speculation that then can be made is that perhaps the isolated, solitary activity of self-harm performs the function of a mistaken and ultimately faulty variation of an adolescent girl's puberty rite. In this context it is an initiation rite with no lasting regeneration and no meaningful connection with knowledge, sexuality or spiritual insight. The behaviour is not approved, nor is it part of a wider social system. In that sense it is confused and misinformed, and finally destructive.

The anthropological literature also gives interesting evidence of mutilation of body parts specifically as part of health and healing rituals. In one example Powers (1986) notes how the bereaved Oglala North American Indian fathers would cut off their little finger following an infant's death. Similarly the Tonga islanders in the nineteenth century were reputed to have cut off portions of their little fingers for the recovery of sick relatives. Another speculation is that this emphasis on injury as part of a healing process could be seen as a link with the claim of the young women who were cutting themselves that it made them feel better, it released tension and helped them feel 'real' again.

Another motivation for cutting or injuring specific parts of the body, such as the genitals, is linked to sexual pleasure. The Kama Sutra reports that among certain peoples there is a belief that one cannot enjoy truly intense sexual pleasure unless the penis has been perforated. Following piercing, the hole across the penis is enlarged, then ornaments called Apadravyas are attached. This sort of practice undoubtedly can be seen to have a direct link with contemporary genital piercing for sexual pleasure, which is discussed later in this chapter. It is well known that body injury serves as a way of social ordering by distinguishing one group from another, and this is a tradition still adhered to in parts of con-temporary society. Jewish male circumcision is one obvious example. Scarification is another, the deliberate cutting of the skin to produce scars for ethnic differentiation or social and aesthetic reasons. Scar patterns and modifications, such as lip or neck rings, are used to show membership of one tribe or another, or social status within the tribe. As is shown below, this is the rationale for some contemporary body-piercing practices. Another speculation would be that by repeated self-harming some of the young women I have described built up a definition and an identity. In some situations such as residential units or in group work they were able to claim membership of a social grouping – that of those who self-harmed.

Other cutting rituals have served as social healing or as recognition for an entire grouping. In the past, Libyan Amazons, or 'female warriors', cauterised the right breast of girl children so that girls would be better able to handle weapons (Newton and Webster 1976). Favazza (1989: 120) quotes published research based on a study of an Ivory Coast tribe and their powerful New Year festivities. The festivities began when, guided by good spirits that were felt to possess their bodies, tribal members knifed themselves. When the serious stomach wounds were healed through a herbal poultice, the tribal members claimed that both wound and healing were prescribed by the spirits, and that this resulted in the social healing of the community. Favazza (1989) notes generally that rituals often involved the therapeutic use of blood, and links this to the practice of blood-letting, and contemporary practices of blood transfusions. Other well-documented mutilative practices to the body have included Moroccan head slashing, and trephination – the drilling of holes in the head. Finally head-moulding as a specific practice was found among the Native American Indians, and in Europe, especially in France and Holland up until the mid-nineteenth century – one manifestation of self-fashioning.

The archaeological findings are less clear-cut, and are deduced on the whole from physical object remains and traces from burial finds. Despite this, they give further evidence of the idea of cutting either as some form of representation of healing, or as a designation of status that goes back to the earliest times. For example, the bronze clamp found in the River Thames at London Bridge was probably used for ritual castration and mutilation by the priests and worshippers of the goddess Cybele during the Roman occupation (British Museum Trustees 1964). Bahn and Vertut (1988) in their work on images of the Ice Age, discuss hand and forearm stencils found in caves in France, Spain and Italy. Their deduction is that the missing finger bones shown on many of the stencils seem to support a theory of ritual mutilation of the little finger.

A similar deliberate amputation of finger joints also seems to have been widespread in southern African communities, and there is further evidence of tattoos, missing teeth and altered cranial morphology during the Late Ice Age. In their analysis of ritual mutilation in southern Africa, Mitchell and Plug (1997) discuss the use of such practices in later social groups as a form of social control, and suggest that the deliberate cutting off of finger bones may have been used in some societies to reinforce male dominance over women. In some groupings the finger joint amputation was carried out specifically by the father of the female child, and was also seen as a way of avoiding illness or misfortune. In other peoples the amputation denoted ethnic identity, or was used as a way to signal mourning. The excavation of complete skeletons lacking finger joints provides evidence of prehistoric finger removal; one such fascinating find is of a 2700-year-old burial of an adult woman in which all the bones, except a few of the phalanges (finger joints) were recovered. Isolated remains of human hand bones and human foot bones have also been excavated from Later Stone Age sites, but in some cases the position of the bones suggests that the mutilation may have been done following death, and so perhaps have fulfilled the purpose of aiding the individual's passage through to the next world.

The excavation of complete skeletons lacking finger joints provides evidence of prehistoric finger removal and the direct use of human body parts to create medicine administered for healing is documented by Mitchell and Plug (1997). The same authors also cite evidence of ethnographic accounts of scarification and tattooing. Some of these practices have recently been found in contemporary tribal groupings in southern Africa. Both practices may be used to denote gender and ethnic identity, with the marks and tattoos for boys signifying the first killing of a large animal, while the markings on girls seem to be decorative.

All these practices may seem brutal and primitive, and very remote from the experiences of people who harm themselves in contemporary society. Yet it is possible that vestiges of such experiences and systems of thought remain as part of our cultural heritage, and part of our collective awareness. For example, we can speculate on the association between body injury as imposed by the father as a form of social control for females, and the earlier discussions in Chapter 3 on the propensity for many young women to internalise a prohibition and turn their anger and aggression inwards on their own bodies. In a similar way, when the young women spoke about protecting their mothers or families by inflicting these secret injuries on themselves, is it possible that there are echoes in that of sacrifice? Is there not a deep association between the magical belief that strong powers and judgemental forces can be appeased through pain and suffering, and the omnipotence and narcissism of the adolescent mind-set discussed in Chapter 4? Freud reminds us of the magical character of the primary obsessive acts of neurotics when he writes of the need to ward off the neurotic's expectations of disaster. 'The protective formulas of obsessional neuroses, too, have their counterpart in the formulas of magic' (1913: 88).

Religious and historical aspects

The majority of religions contain elements of attacking the body as part of a process both of appeasement of judgemental forces and asceticism. This tends to involve beliefs focused on controlling the senses or the body's appetites, or as it is sometimes described, the process of morti-fication of the flesh. Many of the major religions include stories, myths, practices and rituals that involve violence, sacrifice, suffering, martyrdom and the shedding of blood associated with healing, salvation and social order. The very earliest creation myths involve the idea of sacrifice and mutilation usually of a god, such as the Egyptian god Osiris, the Phrygian god Attis and the Greek god Dionysos. Leeming refers to these as 'divine scapegoats' (1994: 58), who are dismembered in order to begin new creations, so from their sacrifice the world and social order are created. The spilling and drinking of sacrificial blood carries powerful symbolism and is present in the earliest religious movements, and repeated in Christianity with the poignant picture of the destruction and slaughter of the sacrificial lamb, whose spilt blood can heal and renew.

In this context there is a strong creative as well as healing aspect to the injuries, and again one can speculate on the link between this and the particular configuration of the encaptive conflict where cutting can be seen as in some ways an expressively creative 'solution' to the intense psychic conflict. As with some of the initiation rites, some religious practices involve injuries and painful actions that are inflicted by the individuals themselves, while other behaviours are willingly or even eagerly submitted to. The harming or mutilation represents control and sacrifice, and often the sacrifice demanded is of the aspirant's sexual life. Here too we can conjecture on the connection with the turbulence and confusion of powerful sexual impulses particularly during adolescence that may contribute to the need to cut.

Ritualised cutting is documented in the Old Testament, where there is a description of part of a religious ceremony by the prophets of Baal. 'They . . . as was their custom, gashed themselves with swords and spears until the blood ran' (1 Kings 18:28). Here it seems that the experience of attacking the body had a direct link to seeking appeasement, or humbling oneself in some way. In the New Testament one of the miracles of Jesus' ministry is given in Mark Chapter 5, and involved his treatment of a man who was uncontrollable and cutting himself: 'And so, unceasingly, night and day, he would cry aloud among the tombs and on the hill-sides and cut himself with stones' (Mark 5:5). Jesus' solution involved commanding the unclean spirits to leave the man, and two thousand of these spirits entered into a nearby herd of pigs who drowned – demonstrating the extent and the power of the uncontrollable impulses. The biblical passage 'If your right eye is your undoing, tear it out and fling it away. . . . And if your right hand is your undoing, cut it off' (Matthew 5:29, 30) has often been taken literally rather than symbolically. Here we see the power of attacking the body both as a form of punishment and the route to the forgiveness of sins. This frequently quoted injunction has provided the basis for many incidents of mutilation, both individually and collectively. It directly led to the foundation of the often quoted Skoptsi sect from Russia. This began in 1757, reaching 150,000 members, all of whom practised varying degrees of self-mutilation and castration as a way of reaching salvation. In Chapter 3, self-harm as a form of self-punishment was explored. While the young women at the clinic were clearly not searching for salvation through their injuries, they were unconsciously trying to save and deliver themselves from the pain of the encaptive conflict and their experienced enslavement to an inner tyrannical and conflictual object relationship.

In Christianity mortification of the flesh has generally been an important theme. For example, by flagellation the body is punished, especially for sexual feelings, and by fasting the body is controlled. This is done by the person for their own salvation, though indirectly it is seen as benefiting society. Cross (1993), in her description of the seriously distorted eating habits among the 'holy women' of medieval Europe, notes that these women, who practised extreme fasting and purging of their bodies, enjoyed social prestige and even power. She points out that this is in sharp contrast to the impotent self-destruction of contemporary anorexic and self-cutting women.

The lives of the Desert Fathers who lived in solitude in the Egyptian desert in the fourth century CE were seen as a model of asceticism. The way to salvation was through ridding the body of all passions and desires, and echoed the saying of Dorotheus the Theban: 'I kill my body, for it kills me.' Underhill's (1960) valuable study of mysticism clarifies that the primary object of mortification is the death of selfhood, in its narrow individualistic sense. Here paradoxically is an attack by the self as a route to subduing the self. Pain is therefore welcomed and sought. She describes the experience of Madame Guyon, 'a delicate girl of the leisured class', who 'characteristically chose the most crude and immoderate forms of mortification in her efforts towards the acquirement of "indifference"' (1960: 225). Underhill quotes from Guyon's own haunting account:

> Although I had a very delicate body, the instruments of penitence tore my flesh without, as it seemed to me, causing pain. I wore girdles of hair and of sharp iron, I often held wormwood in my mouth. . . . If I walked I put stones in my shoes.
>
> (Underhill 1960: 226)

'It has to hurt, really hurt, I thought, or else how can it work. . . . It was not just my body I wanted to hurt; it was myself' (1981: 183). In her fascinating description of contemporary life as a nun, Armstrong (1981) writes of mortifying the body, putting it to death, initially through eating things she did not like and later regular fasting, and also through flagellation. In her account she remembers St Paul's words 'I buffet my body and make it my slave', and is instructed to use the small whip of knotted cords as a way of attempting to subdue her unruly body and its instincts. The whip bruises and cuts her body. Armstrong finds that the result of such extreme pain is an excitement, and arousal of her flesh – the auto-erotic aspects of self-harming are seen emerging here. However, on confiding this to her superior she is instructed to beat herself harder, and increase her fasting. For both Madame Guyon and Karen Armstrong the body injuries were a route for transformation involving a transcendent aspect and serious and devoted religious beliefs. The young women who were cutting certainly wanted to change how they were feeling, but their actions were intrinsically narcissistic and omnipotent, with an element of auto-eroticism.

It is clear from this brief overview that attacking the body by cutting or hitting is a practice that has existed from the earliest times. Is it possible that this cultural experience is stored somewhere, consciously and/or unconsciously, in our psyche? Freud thought so when he wrote about phylogenetic endowment, and the idea that the individual reaches beyond his own experience into primeval experiences: 'the psychology of the neuroses has stored up in it more of the antiquities of human development than any other source' (1917: 371). Jung (1927/31) reflected further on such possibilities, and his concept of the collective unconscious posited an inherited substratum prior to consciousness. He suggests that contained in this is the inherited mass of human development which is somehow represented in each individual cerebral structure. The collective unconscious can be seen to articulate itself in potentialities and possible representations that repeat typical human psychic experiences. Undoubtedly, despite these deep patterns or inborn potentialities, each of us creates our individual world from our interaction with our environment – including our relationships with the people around us and our culture. Yet is it possible that in situations of confused turbulence and conflict some archaic experiences break through and help to form an apparent solution? In the context of this discussion, archetypal potentialities and the archetypal images generated would include those of initiation, sacrifice and salvation. Perhaps cutting can be seen as an activity somehow connected to this deeper level of archetypal experience.

There is some confirmation for this possibility when Podvoll (1969), using different terminology, suggests that the history of images of self-harming reaches at least as far back as the Passion of the Cross. There are many powerful images, some still present in contemporary culture. Therefore, given that self-harming has prevailed among some of the most respected members of our culture, it is understandable that such patterns of behaviour already exist within the person's social field. Whether within the social field, or as part of the collective unconscious, the experience of deliberately hurting the body is an aspect of our common heritage and culture, deeply embedded in the most basic experiences of religion and social custom. It touches upon the profound human and universal experiences of salvation, healing and orderliness. If this is the case then that is true for all of us, but there have to be particular predispositions in those who access these potentialities, using them for their own needs rather than as part of a wider set of social or religious belief systems. It is here that the individual aspects of the encaptive conflict and the internalised object relations come into play, alongside the adolescent mind-set.

Social and cultural aspects

In this section I briefly explore contexts where self-harming is recognised and either partially or wholly seen as acceptable and in some ways understandable, and then try to comprehend if and how this differs from the manifestation among the young women seen for psychotherapy.

It is well recognised that self-harm, particularly cutting, is prevalent in some crowded institutional settings, with particularly high incidence rates among female prisoners (Home Office 1999). It is not that this is seen as an acceptable state of affairs, but for various reasons this worrying tendency appears to evoke less horror and concern than when it occurs in the community. Why is this so? To a certain extent this may be partly a case of 'out of sight is out of mind'. In addition, various dismissive stereotypes and critical judgements tend to be given to people in prison. It has also been suggested that people in institutions who self-harm are silenced and so their distress is not really heard, rather they are seen as 'fundamentally faulty and in need of correction' (Bristol Crisis Service for Women 1995b: 14). One direct reason has been established for the high frequency in institutions, and this is linked to the immediate environmental setting. Incarceration, even in an overcrowded prison, leads to feelings of isolation and frustration. This same reason has been linked to head-banging behaviour in children who are sensory deprived or severely intellectually impaired.

The findings are in part drawn from inhumane animal research with monkeys isolated for long periods, where it was demonstrated that the monkeys began to attack and 'fight' one of their own limbs; this behaviour was then interpreted as a way of self-stimulating to counteract boredom. Similar research showed that monkeys reared from an early age in social isolation often became what is termed 'adult automutilators' – scratching, biting and gouging any accessible body tissue (Favazza 1996: 77). Jones (1979), in a study directly linking animal and human self-harming behaviour, found that cutting, as distinct from other methods, is the nearest to the biting and scratching of animals, both for the precipitating event of bond disruption of some sort, and for the physiological value of tension reduction. In other words, self-harm functions as a way of dealing with the loneliness, loss of close relations and the frustration and boredom of being locked up.

How different is this from the young women in the community? For those in institutions there appears to be an actual external enactment of aspects of the encaptive conflict – imprisoned and unable to break free from the overwhelming and tyrannical power of the state (mother/abuser) who controls one's freedom, and yet at the same time offering a form of security and safety to which, through misguided actions, one is drawn.

Contemporary manifestations of other forms of body injury include tattooing and body piercing – activities that are on the edge of social acceptability and understanding. They have meaning as ways either of expressing individuality or as part of identifying and associating with others and a specific group. Both piercing and tattooing are practices that show the preoccupation around body flesh and a sense of self-image. The person who inscribes on their body in this context is wanting the injury to be seen, and for themselves to be categorised and recognised as a certain sort of person. In this context the body is the site for some form of self-realisation and statement about the self. It is a form of overt self-fashioning.

Unlike the young women cutting alone, attacking the body in this context provides a sense of stability and social cohesion, and such rituals can help a group define themselves apart from other social groupings, and can mark initiation into a different stage of life, rather like the initiation rituals described above. Tattooing is a ritual used in this way, and has its roots in antiquity. References are found of tattooed Egyptian mummies, early Britons and Roman soldiers. Leviticus (19:28) prohibits both cutting of the body and tattooing. There is a tradition of using tattoos to brand and categorise. For example, concentration camp prisoners were tattooed with a number by the Nazis, deserters in the British army were marked with a D and 'bad characters' branded with a BC. Nowadays this use of tattooing has been taken up by nonconformist groups as a way of showing their defiance of traditional authority; thus, for example, many male prisoners in Western jails are tattooed. There is then a link between tattooing and defensive or aggressive aspects of masculinity, but this too is changing. The history of the practice of tattooing reveals two strands – one with the disreputable and marginal members of society, the other with the primitive and exotic tribes of earlier times. In contemporary society the two strands are increasingly interwoven, although, as Benson (2000) points out, in reality tattooing is still associated with the marginal or disempowered.

Body painting emerged in the 1960s as a fun experience signalling sexual freedom and nonconformity. Thirty years on, face paints are an accepted part of children's play. Similarly the popularity of body piercing in the late twentieth century emerged from America, and started in the mid- to late 1970s in the San Francisco gay community, where it was initially linked to leather fetishes and sado-masochistic activities. By the late 1970s body piercing became popular among punks both in the United States and Britain. Although initially starting as an underground practice, by the 1990s body piercing began to appear as part of the musical subculture and alternative fashion scene. Full-time piercing and tattooing studios were opening by the mid-1990s, providing a consumer service available to all adults. Piercing now has its own form of discourse, media outlets and a high level of visibility. In that sense it is seen as socially acceptable, though beyond a certain point it generally becomes associated with the bizarre or perverse.

However, despite being visible and conscious, piercing and tattooing the body do still place the person 'outside society'. Benson interestingly writes that these practices 'transform or negate something central about the kind of person demanded by "society" in late capitalism' (2000: 242). She suggests that the transformation is achieved primarily by the link with the primitive and atavistic. The person who pierces or tattoos their body can then identify with something authentic and pure – something that is anti-repressive and not controlling. In this way the meaning attributed to what the person has externally done to the body surface can be internalised and owned as part of the self. In this context the breaking free of the power of the state (mother/abuser) is openly displayed in order to gain a reaction. Both tattooing and body piercing begin as controlled, socially permitted activities intended to be seen and acknowledged. Among body piercers there are some who view body manipulations as transformative experiences, and call themselves neo-tribalists or modern primitives.

The body parts most often pierced both by women and men are the face, navel, nipples and genitals, and there are a variety of conscious reasons for doing this. The obvious ones include fashion and aesthetics: face piercing of ears, lips, nose and eyebrows both makes a statement about the person and can be seen as a fashion accessory. Ear piercing is the most common form of mild mutilation and is found throughout the world, and in all times. Nipple and genital piercing may partly be done for sensual pleasure and as a way of adding sexual sensation. A body ring may mark a special event in someone's life, or act as a symbol of commitment or possession in a relationship. It may also represent a way or signifier of reclamation, for example, for a survivor of abuse. While some people endure the piercing process for the final result, others may enjoy the painful sensation with the associated release of endorphins.

I was expecting a very painful experience . . . rather I have hardly noticed any pain from it. For the first few days it was so intensely pleasurable I had trouble concentrating – it was a perfect intimate touching exactly the right place . . . I'm delighted with the piercing, and recommend it highly to everyone who has the right anatomy for it. . . . It also goes beautifully with the clit hood piercing, which is also horizontal with a matching ring . . . I am thinking of getting another . . . so that I will have a set of three rings in a row.

(Greenblatt 1999: 10b,1)

Is this socially acceptable? Clearly partially so; however, there are also perverse and destructive elements connected to inflicting so much pain on the body. It is here that the link lies with the young women who self-harm, but again the subjective perspective is different. The young women were rarely celebrating their sexuality; rather they were feeling guilty, confused and distressed by these instinctual processes.

This social and cultural backdrop to attacking the body can help us place the behaviour in a wider context, reminding us of life outside the consulting room. It is now time to draw together the various strands identified and developed in this book, and this will be the task of the final chapter.

Chapter 8

Concluding thoughts

After leaving the clinic there was time and space for me to reflect on the nature of self-harming behaviour, and the impact on me of the level of distress the young women had brought to their psychotherapy sessions. Their frequent presentation of their symptoms as some sort of effective and satisfactory way of managing was reinforced by the experiences and literature from several community-based projects and self-help groups. In some of the literature from these projects there seemed to be an implicit message almost advocating 'a woman's right to cut and injure herself', and an acceptance that self-harm was a convincing way of coping with distress. Yet the question remained: Why was it that so many young women wanted or needed to repeatedly inflict this sort of damage on themselves? How could this possibly appear, and repeatedly appear, to be a valid and sound way of managing feelings? These sorts of questions and dilemmas were posed at the start of this book, and provided the impetus for thinking about trying to understand the meanings behind the symptom.

The search for meaning and knowledge about the world we live in is a fundamental force. There is a basic need to understand suffering and to try to make sense of it in ourselves and others, perhaps even more so when it is self-inflicted, accepted and justified. This search to understand the meanings behind the self-destructive symptoms of the young women with whom I worked might be seen as some form of defensive manoeuvre on my part. After all, the repetitive cutting at times appeared so random, triggered by some apparently trivial and avoidable occurrence, that it was a temptation to dismiss and belittle the symptoms, or just see it as some sort of histrionic attention seeking. Alternatively it might be merely understood as a strange but valid way that the young person had found of managing – after all it was not going to kill them: there were worse and more dangerous methods, some of which they also used. Perhaps the very nature of the cutting felt an aggressive and dismissive slight on the psychotherapeutic task and method of establishing a relationship. Yet the actions also provoked high anxiety among the other professionals both inside and outside the clinic setting. Even the most hardened and experienced clinicians found the apparently mindless violence of repeated cutting extremely daunting and frustrating.

As has been demonstrated in this book, the experience and clinical material from the young women who were seen for psychotherapy did over time reveal some understanding of the dynamics and meanings involved in self-harming. Initially patients such as Anne, Diana, Laura and Lucy and the others I mention were inhabiting private worlds where their agony was intrasubjective, their shame and secrecy precluded sharing, and their inhibitions were strong. From my position as therapist I recognised that the private can become public and intersubjective, and that personal experience can lead to understanding the agony of another. When the young women who were harming themselves began to, and were able to, experience me as listening, even if very little was actually being said, then I think a transformation started to take place in the relations between the unconscious and consciousness.

The therapist 'knows' and understands about listening to the conscious and unconscious language of the patient, yet the knowledge comes not from the literature or training courses but from the therapist's own analysis, which has to be effective and intensive enough to enable them to listen to the analysis of others. The thinking about the patient is a form of understanding from experience, an inside vantage point that then involves thinking from a plurality of perspectives. In other words, analytic thought, theory and reasoning about meanings emerges from our subjectivity. It is a partial perspective which includes when, where and how we position ourselves. Analytic meanings emanate from thinking and theorising about subjective and specific experiences, and remain a sort of story-telling no matter how they are couched in abstract terms and complicated language. So in part this account has been the story-telling of my relationships with the young women I met in the clinic and the others I encountered who were harming themselves, and the stories they told.

My thinking has also clearly been affected by the thinking and theories of others. The theoretical knowledge and ideas raised by others working in the same and related fields has acted as a base for the embodiment of experiential knowledge – the internalisation of the analytic person and process. Embodied knowledge and understanding is partial in that it is about living within the limits and contradictions of our own ability to experience. It is about a knowing from within. However, it can feel like knowledge that we are often unaware of possessing, except in practice, so that thinking theoretically about the patient is often a different experience from thinking in the presence of the patient.

For knowledge and meaning to be analytic it must remain a supposition, always dynamic and open to questioning and testing. There is an inherent contradiction between pinning down meaning and the shock of the raw and primitive nature of the unconscious, with the awareness that the unconscious can only be brought to a limiting and shifting level of conscious control. The meanings and understanding of any behaviour and symptoms in another person have to remain provisional and speculative, and any reasoning balanced by the awareness of the unconscious as disruptive and unpredictable. The prerequisite for gaining some understanding of the meaning involves listening, as mentioned earlier, and a level of receptivity to what is going on in the therapy and with the patient, which is dependent on the quality of the therapist's evenly suspended attention. Within such awareness lies recognition of the dynamics of the transference and countertransference. Indeed it is essentially from the transference and countertransference relationship that some sense can be made. This can in turn hopefully lead to understanding and so to therapeutic insight.

My contention in this book has been that at the heart of the transference experiences lies an internal constellation particular to those who are harming themselves. This I have termed 'the encaptive conflict'. From the dynamics of the therapeutic work with the young women there gradually emerged a sense of a central unconscious psychic formation common in its basic configuration to each of them, although different in its particular individual manifestation. In thinking about this I understood it as a variant and possibly perverse side formation of the core complex described by Glasser (1992). My suggestion was that instead of fusion with an idealised mother as in the core complex, the encaptive conflict involves the captivation by an avaricious object who overwhelms, and from whom there is ambivalence and anxiety about separation.

Anne, whose difficulties and psychotherapy I have described in some detail, summed up her experiences in this way:

A prisoner behind invisible bars,
filled deep with emotional scars,
trapped forever by my mind,
peace within I cannot find.

She spoke of her state of mind as a 'life sentence', where the 'prison gates were too high' and 'the key had been thrown away'. A state where the fear of being possessed conflicted with the fear of rejection and the psychic conflict led to a defensive compromise. The solution to the conflict was hostility, which was turned inwards against the self and the body, rather than directed outwards on to an external object. It is this intrapsychic dynamic that repeatedly fuelled the attacks on the body.

The encaptive conflict appears to be strongest at the developmental stages where separation is a central concern. Adolescence is clearly one such stage, and as I have suggested in Chapter 4, self-harming is partially dependent on what I have termed 'an adolescent mind-set', where characteristics such as narcissism, aggression, hypersensitivity and omnipotence are heightened. I have proposed that if the conflict can become more conscious, understood and worked through then its power wanes. This raises the question of what happens to those who are cutting themselves in adolescence and who are not able to resolve their difficulties. Certainly some continue to cut well into early adulthood, but it does appear that only a small number continue to do so in middle age and beyond. My contention is that those, such as Martha, described in Chapter 3, are still stranded in an adolescent state of mind, and issues of separation – perhaps especially from mother – remain unresolved. Others I would propose gradually adopt alternative symptoms that fulfil the same release of tension or diversion from the same inner unconscious encaptive conflict. These symptoms would not be seen as self-harming in the accepted sense, but are none the less an attack on the body – perhaps forming as panic attacks, hypochondriasis, or various masochistic behaviours.

In Chapter 1 I brought up the idea that the meanings behind attacking the body can be found through thinking of the attack as a paradoxical gesture; as metaphorical representation; and as symbolic action. In this chapter I want to pull together these thoughts and see if a model can be established for containing the different meanings explored in this book. Obviously the encaptive conflict would lie at the heart of this model.

Alongside the ideas of paradox, metaphor and symbolism are the words gesture, representation and action. At the most obvious level these actions of attacking the body as a way of feeling better or relieving tension have to appear as gestures. Among the young women whom I worked with, cutting ultimately perpetuated the distress and certainly only relieved it for a short time. However, as a gesture it was full of paradox. Against all apparent common-sense thinking, the destruction turned out to be constructive in the minds of those inflicting the damage. The attacks that seemed to be about wanting to hurt, cut out and destroy had meaning in the sense that they provided a way of continuing to live. As mentioned, it was clear that for many of the young women the actions were their solution to having difficult, disturbing and uncontrollable sensations and feelings. In this way, the self-destructive symptom was in itself undoubtedly experienced as a form of 'self-help' and 'self-survival' – a meaning confirmed by the literature and conference reports from community networks. The young women who cut themselves understood their actions as a way of managing, although as referral to counselling or psychiatric services confirmed, sometimes the solution became the problem – and of course was usually seen that way by family, friends and professionals. For some of the young women, the emotional pain and suffering felt unremitting and sometimes incomprehensible – they often did not know why they felt so terrible. All they knew was that they needed to repeatedly cut and so the harming became their whole life. Attacking the body was both constructing and restricting their lives, and defining who they were as well as what they did.

It appeared that paradox also inevitably lay at the heart of the encaptive conflict: an inner connection that both captivated and from which there was both the fear and the longing to separate. Among the young women seen, it involved an inner dependency that was at the same time both terrifying and attractive. As long as the conflict remained unconscious the feelings of love and hate stayed split, and it was not possible to allow both feelings to co-exist in a state of ambivalence. The fantasies attached to cutting were also often paradoxical, yet they were always meaningful. When these fantasies were spoken about by the young women they tended to be about ongoing relationships – of the rather immediate 'they'll be sorry' variety – a settling of a recent injury to the self by a present physical injury to the body. Yet the perpetrator usually remained ignorant of what was happening in their name. At a deeper level the fantasy resonated with the internalised processes derived from much earlier object relations, revealing both the attraction and repulsion to a terrifying intimacy.

Another paradoxical aspect was that attacking the body – like most other symptoms – served as a protection for the inner self. It served as a defence against these deeper, earlier, unbearable or catastrophic emotional attacks. The defence was triggered by something more recent and usually much less significant, but which was an unconscious reminder of an earlier experience. The young women were in some senses psycho-logically reliving infancy, when separation issues and a sense of self were central. The symptom appeared at times to be an attempt at maintaining or repairing the cohesiveness of the self, in the presence or the wake of the great anxiety or distress caused by psychic conflict. The fear and anxiety was that the self might disappear under the pressure of the unconscious conflict, so the more conscious ego employed the symptom, and the resulting pain stimulated and established a frontier which included safe and familiar territory.

The cutting in itself constituted a line between the unconscious conflict and the conscious sensations. It gave the pain a shape and an edge. At the same time the line of blood was the link between the conscious and unconscious processes – it was the meeting place where uncontained mental pain could be transformed into manageable physical pain. When this was repeated, the razor and the cutting became the reliable companion. It is therefore no wonder that the symptom was owned as a satisfactory way of managing. However, the danger, and a further paradox, was that the symptom apparently used so successfully by the ego to protect the self in the manner described could take over, and like the most intrusive of companions, overwhelm. Then it stopped providing a boundary, and seemed to take possession of the self. This was the case among the young women who defined themselves solely through their history of self-harm and their plans for and interest in future self-destructive actions. Therefore in a further paradox, the solution that had been found to manage the awful sensations emerging from the unconscious encaptive conflict became the conscious dominating strategy for being and living – so re-enacting the inner drama it was trying to control.

Another of the paradoxical gestures about cutting the surface of the skin was that the selection of skin surface by the young women could be seen in part as a compensation for the lack of more intimate contact during infancy. In that sense the skin was the memorial for this deprivation, and in turn was the place for the memories to re-emerge and be replayed. The wounds became the route of remembrance. Cutting also provided a way of finding comfort, solace and excitement, and in that way could also be viewed as a form of auto-eroticism and masturbation. A further paradoxical aspect was that in performing these private attacks, the young women gradually found a public voice. The silent actions, which took place in such secrecy, became the route into the public domain and eventually into the world of words.

In the chapters about clinical work there was a focus on the ways in which the specific meaning for each person could be uncovered and eventually spoken about. This was always through the building up of the therapeutic relationship. Some of the difficulties specific to working with young people were also discussed. One such difficulty was when there was an inability to put sensations into feelings and thoughts. Another was when feelings were repressed, or dissociated. Often the young person needed firm encouragement to begin to put their emotions into words in the presence of another, whom they could trust and who was interested in understanding them. Sometimes this happened through thinking about dreams. Occasions arose when the young patient needed a more authoritative intervention, and times when the therapist needed to take on the caring function. In other situations the patient was seen as too unstable to cope with analytic work and insight, and needed instead a supportive relationship, or occasionally even the safety of a hospital or residential unit.

Psychoanalytic psychotherapy is essentially a radical project, in that it eschews the superficial conventions of behaviour, above all adopting the belief that 'things are not what they seem'. In that sense every piece of clinical work is a chance to look below the surface appearances at what is beneath, and unravel the paradoxical aspects.

Cutting is also a metaphoric representation. What does this mean? A metaphor is a figure of speech. One of the central themes has been that the attacks demonstrated the inability of the young women to verbally represent their feelings. If feelings cannot be put into words then actions have to carry the direct meaning, and represent the inner state of mind. Thus as a metaphoric representation, the attack on the body represented an inner state of mind that could not be spoken about. This was partly because it was inaccessible through being unconscious, and partly because either repression or dissociation prevented the conflict from emerging into conscious awareness. The inner state of mind is the encaptive conflict – an apparently irreconcilable and unconscious psychic conflict involving a specific type of inner object relationship. As discussed above, the details will be different for each individual, but there is a common formation of enslavement and the longing to break free.

Unravelling and exploring the encaptive conflict and how it evolved is the task of the therapy. In this way there can be a gradual understanding and breaking free from the strong bonds of ambivalence. In the exploration of the link between an adolescent state of mind and self-harm in Chapter 4, attention was drawn to two central characteristics – gaining a sexual identity and separation–individuation. For some of those young women the captivation with a tyrannical and avaricious inner object seemed to link back to earlier problems involving separation from their mothers. These earlier states had been reactivated by the pressures and demands of adolescence. The young women needed and wanted to break free but seemed to be held back by a longing for the fusion. The cutting symbolised the captive state, but could also have further meaning as a metaphoric representation of a misplaced attack on the internalised mother in the struggle to break free. The cutting metaphorically represented this and the ambivalence over the separation.

For others, there also appeared to be a link to a powerful, abusive figure replicating an earlier abuser–abused dyad. This was sometimes linked to direct abusive traumas, and this was explored in Chapter 3. Again, the desire to escape was countered by the terror of separation. The encaptive conflict was augmented and fuelled by instinctual processes that had been affected by the external experiences, but too often the violent aggression was turned back on the self. External wounding has meaning as a metaphoric representation of an inner wound – but the nature of the wound and understanding the connection with the external environment can emerge in therapy. The symptom can be seen to represent both the enslavement and an attack on that enslavement, and the desire to cut loose and the punishment for that desire. Consciously the violence appears to be under the control of the young woman, and directed at her volition against her own body.

One of the findings cited was that young people who have had a neglectful and deprived early childhood are less likely to care for their bodies. Aspects of parental handling or the lack of it are transferred into the psyche, so affecting the way the young person ends up caring for herself. For cutting to take place the body has to be conceived as something other and alien, something that can be treated with contempt, but that is still connected to the self. This means that the relationship with the body is one of disconnection and not integration. Partly because the young women had learned through different experiences to rely on themselves, external relationships were mostly treated with suspicion. There was a strong attachment to the inner object relations which were based on destruction. The safe relationship had become that with the objects used – the knife and razor. These objects came to represent comfort and reassurance. In some situations, described in Chapter 2, the objects became the focus for ritual and an obsessional form of ceremony. As well as providing comfort, the auto-erotic aspects involved in repeated and addictive cutting also substituted and served as a perverted form of 'maternal' care.

As described in Chapter 1, at the clinic there were no young men cutting themselves – it generally seemed to be a female symptom. Despite thirty years of public awareness of assertiveness training, there appeared to be an obvious difficulty for the young women seen in openly acknowledging and directly expressing aggression. The muted aggression re-emerged as self-preservative violence, directed inwards against the self and on to the body. 'Letting rip' on her own skin could be seen as a sign that something 'incisive' needed to happen in order to deal with the un-manageable feelings emerging from the encaptive conflict. As discussed above, the 'right' to cut and injure the body is fought for so fiercely by some as apparently the only way to manage. As women and girls we are disempowered in so many ways, and in so many situations, and this includes the ownership of our bodies. Superficial mastery and owner-ship is reclaimed by the attack, although the anger is misdirected, and ultimately increases the feelings of impotency and meaninglessness.

Attacking the body is both a symptom and a symbolic action, and like both symptoms and symbols needs to be 'read'. Perhaps this almost seems easier to do when we look back at the earliest socially sanctioned practices of self-harm. In early times attacking the surface of the body held a direct known meaning and approved social function, usually for the purposes of initiation, sacrifice and healing. In Chapter 7 various speculations were made about the historical, social and cultural aspects of self-harm. Undoubtedly, knowing about the social and cultural helps position the behaviour. Of course it is of no direct help to the dis-tressed young women, and not of immediate help to the clinician or the concerned relative, to know about these other manifestations. However, in Chapter 7 I raised the possibility that the behaviour so prevalent during adolescence could have additional meanings linked to these cultural aspects.

One hypothesis was that possibly at a collective level there was a deeper resonance linked to archetypal possibilities of initiation and salvation. Self-harm belongs to an adolescent mind-set, and perhaps self-harm has become a contemporary ordeal to find meaning, an initiation into a longed-for different state of mind. There is a desperate desire for real change and regeneration, to escape from the encaptive conflict, but the perverse activity leads to degeneration and to an eventual dead-end. The history of sacrifice and initiation shows that losing a small amount of blood represents a symbolic death leading to the birth of something new. To gain something new some other part has to be relinquished. Although self-harm can be seen as a symbolic action it ultimately fails. Nothing is relinquished through the action; the symptom acts as a form of containment, rather than an opening out into new possibilities and change. The sacrifice does not work, and salvation and healing are not found through attacking the body. Instead of a cleansing and an opening into the future life of potential and possibilities in the individual, the action ultimately further enslaves and overwhelms the sense of self, and no lasting relief is found.

It is clear that there are multi-layered meanings for each individual in attacking their body. How can all these ideas be held in mind? My suggestion in this chapter is for an imaginary model for understanding self-harm based on a conception of four layers. On the top layer is self-harm as a gesture. Here are the conscious reasons or meanings given by the young women for the attacks – it relieves tension, makes me feel real and alive, gets rid of horrible feelings and so on. These also often contain the paradoxical aspects.

The layer below this comprises the meanings or reasons that are not quite conscious, but which can be easily brought to mind, rather like Freud's early model of the pre-conscious. This would include the trigger for the event, such as the slight, the paranoid meeting with someone, a criticism, what was felt immediately before or after the cutting. This layer gives a glimpse of what the deeper concerns might be about. In the third layer are the contents of the personal unconscious, which are often dissociated or repressed. In these second and third layers self-harm is a form of representation. In the third layer lie the unconscious metaphoric meanings. These are to be found in the psychic conflict and the processes internalised from early experiences, and the way that instinctual drives and needs evolved and were affected. The resulting dynamics can become partially accessible, become conscious and understood through the therapeutic relationship and the transference. Here is placed the encaptive conflict, which is inevitably diffused by – though also associated with – the two top layers. Undoubtedly, some of the earliest experiences cannot be retrieved or assimilated, but there will be a sense of the form of the disturbance. It is at these levels that the healing and resolution of the conflict can potentially take place through the psychotherapeutic relationship.

In the deepest layer are aspects of the collective consciousness and collective unconscious with its articulations of archetypal images of initiation and of healing. These archetypal representations may be conceived of as organisers of experience, which can be generated particularly during times of transition, such as adolescence with all the upheaval of sexuality and separation. Potentially in this way there is compensation for what is missing in the personal unconscious. It is as if there is some sense of an unconscious cultural formation that emerges to shape this solution to distress. The individual person is left within their own private pain and story, but is none the less searching for a mythical form for what has felt impossible, irreconcilable and uncontrollable. There would be no conscious awareness of these deeper aspects in the person who is harming themselves.

Although I have described a neat model for the purpose of this discussion, inevitably the various layers and their contents appear in a mixture, and there is a continuous shifting and movement within the person. The model is also affected by its position within contemporary culture. This then includes the issues and constraints around female development and expression, and the contemporary interest in body piercing and tattooing.

Verbal symbols leading to metaphor

Psychotherapy offers the opportunity to bring some parts of the personal unconscious into conscious awareness. Potentially it can transform the paradoxical gesture of self-harm as self-healing into verbal symbols – words – for which a metaphor can then be created. Attacking the body is a symbolic action, but the aim of the talking cure – both counselling and psychotherapy – is to encourage the use of different symbols – the use of words – so that over time talking about feelings becomes a substitute for the earlier destructive action that was necessary to deal with uncomfortable sensations. The power of the conflict lessens, although it is always possible that it might reappear in certain stressful phases. Words can replace wounds, and the person who has been attacking her body as a muted form of communication and comfort can find her own full voice.

Talking about the feelings within the context of a psychotherapeutic relationship can start to serve some of the same conscious functions as the attack, such as relieving tension, being in touch with anger, and ultimately also can link back to healing and well-being. It can also change a perverted form of self-fashioning into a genuine sense of self-worth. Talking about something gives meaning, and in the end it is meaning and the understanding of that meaning that leads to insight and the relief of suffering. Verbal symbols can also become metaphors when the person can think about her feelings, and speak about her need to metaphorically cut out or kill off inner pain, and evacuate all the bad feelings of anger and distress.

It is through the relationship with the psychotherapist, and the dynamics of that relationship, that the painful feelings can be contained, interpreted and ultimately given their specific meaning – and where the experience of searching for meaning can become one of reciprocity. Guntrip summarises this experience beautifully when he writes:

> What is psychoanalytic psychotherapy? It is, as I see it, the provision of a reliable and understanding human relationship of a kind that

makes contact with the deeply repressed traumatised child in a way that enables one to become steadily more able to live, in the security of a new real relationship, with the traumatic legacy of the earliest formative years, as it seeps through or erupts into consciousness.

(Hazell 1994: 366)

It is in transference and countertransference that aspects of the encaptive conflict can gradually emerge and be understood. The repeated cutting ultimately only compounds and deepens the link with the tyrannical inner figure characteristic of the encaptive conflict. The ties that bind are strengthened rather than loosened by the cutting. Psychoanalytic psychotherapy creates the opportunity to understand these inner processes. It allows for the gradual awareness that there is more than one feeling so that there can be some healing of the split between love and hate. The cutting emphasises and marks the splitting – the therapy can potentially heal this wound. One metaphor would be that the bleeding wounds become faded scars as the individual dynamics and ambivalence are understood and given meaning.

Knowing what is meant by a particular symptom, behaviour or feeling carries with it its counterpart, not knowing what is meant – all that lies beneath the meaning. This is of course part of the analytic endeavour, where we are regularly reminded of the power of the unconscious. These unconscious processes are only known if they emerge into consciousness, often doing so as explored through the transference relationship. By definition these processes always include the qualities of surprise, disruption and unpredictability. Not everything is knowable or understandable; instead, the search is about coming to terms with approximations of meaning and approaching what is meant. It is about adding meaning to meaning, and so hopefully providing the next advance into other meanings.

References

Anderson, R. (2000) 'Assessing the risk of self-harm in adolescents', *Psychoanalytic Psychotherapy*, 14, 1: 9–21.

Angelou, M. (1984) *I Know Why the Caged Bird Sings*, London: Virago.

Armstrong, K. (1981) *Through the Narrow Gate*, London: Macmillan.

Bahn, P. G. and Vertut, J. (1988) *Images of the Ice Age*, Leicester: Windward.

Bateman, A. and Holmes, J. (1995) *Introduction to Psychoanalysis*, London and New York: Routledge.

Benson, S. (2000) 'Inscriptions of the self: reflections on tattooing and piercing in contemporary Euro-America', in J. Caplan (ed.) *Written on the Body: The Tattoo in European and American History*, London: Reaktion Books.

Bernstein, D. (1990) 'Female genital anxieties, conflicts and typical mastery modes', *International Journal of Psychoanalysis*, 71: 151–65.

Bettelheim, B. (1955) *The Symbolic Wound*, London: Thames and Hudson.

Bick, E. (1968) 'The experience of the skin in early object-relations', *International Journal of Psychoanalysis*, 49: 484–6.

Bion, W. (1962) 'A theory of thinking', *International Journal of Psychoanalysis*, 43: 306–10.

—— (1967) *Second Thoughts*, London: Karnac.

Biven, B. (1977) 'A violent solution: the role of skin in a severe adolescent regression', *Psychoanalytic Study of the Child*, 32: 327–52.

Blos, P. (1962) *On Adolescence*, New York: The Free Press.

Bollas, C. (1992) *Being a Character*, London and New York: Routledge.

Bovensiepen, G. (1995) 'Suicide and attacks on the body as a containing object', in M. Sidoli and G. Bovensiepen (eds) *Incest Fantasies and Self-Destructive Acts*, New Brunswick and London: Transaction Publishers.

Bristol Crisis Service for Women (1995a) *Women and Self-Injury Report*, Bristol: Bristol Crisis Service for Women.

—— (1995b) *Cutting out the Pain*, Conference proceedings.

British Museum Trustees (1964) *Guide to the Antiquities of Roman Britain*, London.

Britton, R. (1991) 'Keeping things in mind', in R. Anderson (ed.) *Clinical*

Lectures on Klein and Bion, New Library of Psychoanalysis, New York and London: Routledge.

Burnham, R. C. (1969) 'Symposium on impulsive self-mutilation: discussion', *British Journal of Medical Psychology*, 42: 223–9.

Chasseguet-Smirgel, J. (1990) 'On acting out', *International Journal of Psychoanalysis*, 71, 1: 77–86.

Chodorow, N. (1978) *The Reproduction of Mothering*, Berkeley: University of California Press.

—— (1996) 'Nancy Chodorow talks to Anthony Elliott', *Free Associations*, 6, 2 (No. 38): 161–73.

Copley, B. (1993) *The World of Adolescence*, London: Free Association Books.

Cross, L. (1993) 'Body and self in feminine development: implications for eating disorders and delicate self-mutilation', *Bulletin of the Menninger Clinic*, 57, 1: 41–68.

Daldin, H. (1990) 'Self-mutilating behaviour in adolescence with comments on suicidal risk', *Bulletin Anna Freud Centre*, 13: 279–93.

de Young, M. (1982) Self-injurious behaviour in incest victims, *Child Welfare*, 61: 572–84.

Deutsch, H. (1944) *Psychology of Women, Vol.1*, New York: Grune and Stratton, 1945.

Dorey, R. (1986) 'The relationship of mastery', *International Review of Psycho-Analysis*, 13: 323–33.

Easton Ellis, B. (1991) *American Psycho*, London: Picador.

Eliade, M. (1995) *Rites and Symbols of Initiation*, Woodstock, CT: Spring Publications.

Favazza, A. (1989) 'Normal and deviant self-mutilation', *Transcultural Psychiatric Research Review*, 26: 113–27.

—— (1996) *Bodies Under Siege: Self Mutilation and Body Modification In Culture and Psychiatry* (2nd edn), Baltimore, MD: Johns Hopkins University Press.

Fonagy, P. (1991) 'Thinking about thinking: some clinical and theoretical considerations in the treatment of a borderline patient', *International Journal of Psychoanalysis*, 72, 4: 639–56.

—— (1995) 'Psychoanalysis, cognitive-analytic therapy, mind and self', BJP Annual Lecture 1994, *British Journal of Psychotherapy*, 11, 4: 575–84.

Frankel, R. (1998) *The Adolescent Psyche*, London and New York: Routledge.

Freud, A. (1958) 'Adolescence', in *Psychoanalytic Study of the Child* XIII, New York: International University Press.

—— (1968) 'Acting Out', *International Journal of Psychoanalysis*, 49, 2–3: 165–70.

—— (1969) *Normality and Pathology in Childhood*, London: Hogarth Press.

Freud, S. (1895) 'Psychotherapy of hysteria', *Standard Edition* 2, London: Hogarth Press.

—— (1905) 'A case of hysteria', *Standard Edition* 7, London: Hogarth Press.

—— (1907) 'Obsessive actions and religious practices', *Standard Edition* 9, London: Hogarth Press.

—— (1912) 'The dynamics of transference', *Standard Edition* 12, London: Hogarth Press.

—— (1913) 'Totem and taboo', *Standard Edition* 13, London: Hogarth Press.

—— (1914) 'Remembering, repeating and working through', *Standard Edition* 12, London: Hogarth Press.

—— (1915) 'Assessment of the unconscious', *Standard Edition* 14, London: Hogarth Press.

—— (1917a) 'Transference', *Standard Edition* 16, London: Hogarth Press.

—— (1917b) 'The paths to symptom-formation', *Standard Edition* 16, London: Hogarth Press.

—— (1920) 'Beyond the pleasure principle', *Standard Edition* 18, London: Hogarth Press.

—— (1923) 'The ego and the id', *Standard Edition*, 19, London: Hogarth Press.

—— (1924) 'The economic problem of masochism', *Standard Edition*, 19, London: Hogarth Press.

Friedman, M., Glasser, M., Laufer, E., Laufer, M. and Wohl, M. (1972) 'Attempted suicide and self-mutilation in adolescence: some observations from a psychoanalytic research project', *International Journal of Psychoanalysis*, 53: 179–83.

Gabbard, G. (1995) 'Countertransference: the emerging common ground', *International Journal of Psychoanalysis*, 76, 3: 475–86.

Gardner, F. (1990) 'Psychotherapy with adult survivors of child sexual abuse', *British Journal of Psychotherapy*, 6: 285–94.

—— (1999) 'Transgenerational processes and the trauma of sexual abuse', *European Journal of Psychotherapy, Counselling and Health*, 2, 3: 297–308.

—— (forthcoming) 'Dissociation', in A. Scott (ed.) *The Critical Dictionary of Psychoanalytic Thinking*, London and New York: Brunner-Routledge.

Gay, P. (1988) *Freud, A Life for Our Time*, London and Melbourne: J. M. Dent and Sons.

Glasser, M. (1979) 'Some aspects of the role of aggression in the perversions', in I. Rosen (ed.) *Sexual Deviation* (2nd edn), Oxford: Oxford University Press.

—— (1986) 'Identification and its vicissitudes as observed in the perversions', *International Journal of Psychoanalysis*, 67: 9–17.

(1992) 'Problems in the psychoanalysis of certain narcissistic disorders', *International Journal of Psychoanalysis*, 73: 493–504.

—— (1998) 'On violence: a preliminary communication', *International Journal of Pyschoanalysis*, 79, 5: 887–902.

Glenn, J. (1984) 'A note on loss, pain and masochism in children', *Journal of the American Psychoanalytic Association*, 32, 1: 63–73.

Greenberg, H. (1975) 'The widening gyre: transformations of the omnipotent quest during adolescence', *International Review of Psycho-Analysis*, 2: 231–44.

Greenblatt, A. (1999) rec. arts. bodyart: Piercing FAQ, 8 – Historical Information Oxford Universities Libraries Automation Service. Online. Available HTTP: http://www.cs.uu.nl/wais/html/na-dir/bodyart/piercing-faq/.html (13 January 1999).

Grubrich-Simitis, I. (1984) 'From concretism to metaphor', *Psychoanalytic Study of the Child*, 39: 301–19.

Haag, G. (2000) 'In the footsteps of Frances Tustin: further reflections on the construction of the body ego', *Infant Observation*, 3, 3: 7–22.

Haim, A. (1974) *Adolescent Suicide*, London: Tavistock.

Harris, T. (1999) *The Silence of the Lambs*, London: Arrow.

Hazell, J. (1994) *Personal Relations Therapy, The Collected papers of H. J. S. Guntrip*, Northvale, NJ, and London: Jason Aronson.

Heimann, P. (1950) 'On counter-transference', *International Journal of Psychoanalysis*, 31: 81–4.

Hinshelwood, R. D. (1999) 'Countertransference', *International Journal of Psychoanalysis*, 80, 4: 797–818.

Holmes, J. (2000) ' Attachment theory and Psychoanalysis: a rapprochement', *British Journal of Psychotherapy*, 17: 157–172

Home Office (1999) H. M. Chief Inspector of Prisons. *Women in Prison: A Thematic Review*, Appendix 5: 'The health of women prisoners in England and Wales', Online. Available HTTP:
http://www.penlex.org.uk/ciwoma5.html (21 February).

Hopper, E. (1995) 'A psychoanalytical theory of drug addiction', *International Journal of Psychoanalysis*, 76: 1121–42.

Jones, I. (1979) 'A biological approach to two forms of human self-injury', *Journal of Nervous and Mental Diseases*, 16, 2: 74–8.

Joseph, B. (1982) 'Addiction to near-death', *International Journal of Psycho-analysis*, 63: 449–56.

Jung, C. G. (1927/31) *The Structure of the Psyche*, Collected Works 8, London: Routledge & Kegan Paul.

Kafka, J. (1969) 'The body as transitional object: a psychoanalytic study of a self-mutilating patient', *British Journal of Medical Psychology*, 42: 207–12.

Laufer, M. (1982) 'Female masturbation in adolescence and the development of the relationship to the body', *International Journal of Psychoanalysis*, 63: 295–302.

—— (ed.) (1995) *The Suicidal Adolescent*, Connecticut: International Universities Press.

Laufer, M. and Laufer, E. (1984) *Adolescence and Developmental Breakdown*, London: Karnac.

—— (1989) *Developmental Breakdown and Analytic Treatment in Adolescence*, New Haven, CT, and London: Yale University Press.

Leeming, D. (1994) *A Dictionary of Creation Myths*, New York and Oxford: Oxford University Press.

Levenkron, S. (1998) *Cutting*, New York: Norton.

Little, M. (1986) *Transference Neurosis and Transference Psychosis*, London: Free Association Books.

McDougall, J. (1986) *Theatres of the Mind*, London: Free Association Books.

Meissner, W. W. (1992) 'The concept of the therapeutic alliance', *Journal of the American Psychoanalytic Association*, 40: 1059–87.

Menninger, K.(1935) 'A psychoanalytic study of the significance of self-mutilations', *Psychoanalytic Quarterly*, 4: 408–66.

Mitchell, P. J. and Plug, I. (1997) 'Ritual mutilation in Southern Africa', in L. Wadley (ed.) *Our Gendered Past*, Witwatersrand, SA: Witwatersrand University Press.

Montgomery, J. D. and Greif, A. C. (eds) (1989) *Masochism, The Treatment of Self-Inflicted Suffering*, Madison, CT: International Universities Press.

Newton, E. and Webster, P. (1976) 'Matriarchy: as women see it', in S. Cox (ed.) *Female Psychology: The Emerging Self*, Chicago, IL: Science Research Associates.

Orbach, I. (1994) 'Dissociation, physical pain, and suicide: a hypothesis', *Suicide and Life-Threatening Behaviour*, 24, 1: 68–79.

—— (1996) 'The role of body experience in self-destruction', *Clinical Child Psychology and Psychiatry*, 1, 4: 607–19.

Orgel, S. (1974) 'Fusion with the victim and suicide', *International Journal of Psychoanalysis*, 55: 531–8.

Pao, P. (1969) 'The syndrome of delicate self-cutting', *British Journal of Medical Psychology*, 42: 195–205.

Pines, D. (1993) *A Woman's Unconscious Use of the Body*, London: Virago Press.

Pithers, D. (1983) 'What would you say if I fucking nutted you?', Jubilee Conference of the Portman Clinic, *Understanding Human Violence*, September.

Podvoll, E. (1969) 'Self-mutilation within a hospital setting: a study of identity and social compliance', *British Journal of Medical Psychology*, 42: 213–21.

Powers, M. N. (1986) *Oglala Women, Myth, Ritual, and Reality*, Chicago, IL, and London: University of Chicago Press.

Pritchard, C. (1995) *Suicide – The Ultimate Rejection?*, Buckingham: Open University Press.

Ritvo, S. (1984) 'The image and uses of the body in psychic conflict', *Psychoanalytic Study of the Child*, 39: 449–70.

Rosenfeld, H. (1987) *Impasse and Interpretation*, London: Tavistock.

Rosenthal, R., Rinzler, C., Wallsch, R. and Klausner, E. (1972) 'Wrist-cutting syndrome: the meaning of a gesture', *American Journal of Psychiatry*, 128: 1363–8.

Scott, A. (1998a) 'Trauma, skin: memory, speech', in V. Sinason (ed.) *Memory in Dispute*, London: Karnac.

—— (1998b) 'Language as skin', *Trauma and Memory: Cross-Cultural Perspectives*, Conference, Sydney, May.

Segal, H. (1957) 'Notes on symbol formation', *International Journal of Psychoanalysis*, 38: 391–7.

—— (1993) 'On the clinical usefulness of the concept of the death instinct', *International Journal of Psychoanalysis*, 74: 55–62.

Self-Injury Forum Newsletter (1999) 3, Abergavenny: The Basement Project.

Simpson, C. and Porter, G. (1981) 'Self-mutilation in children and adolescents', *Bulletin of the Menninger Clinic*, 45, 5: 428–38.

Steiner, J. (1993) *Psychic Retreats*, London and New York: Routledge.

Strong, M. (2000) *A Bright Red Scream*, London: Virago.

Tantam, D. and Whittaker, J. (1992) 'Personality disorder and self-wounding', *British Journal of Psychiatry*, 161: 451–64.

Tonnesmann, M. (1980) 'Adolescent re-enactment, trauma and reconstruction', *Journal of Child Psychotherapy*, 6: 23–44.

Turp, M. (1999) 'Encountering self-harm in psychotherapy and counselling practice', *British Journal of Psychotherapy*, 15, 3: 306–21.

Underhill, E. (1960) *Mysticism*, London: Methuen.

Van der Kolk, B. A., Perry, C. and Herman, J. L. (1991) 'Childhood origins of self-destructive behaviour', *American Journal of Psychiatry*, 148: 1665–71.

Welldon, E. (1988) *Mother, Madonna, Whore*, London: Free Association Books.

Wilson, P. (1991) 'Psychotherapy with adolescents', in J. Holmes (ed.) *Textbook of Psychotherapy in Psychiatric Practice*, Edinburgh and London: Churchill Livingstone.

Winnicott, D. (1971) *Playing and Reality*, Harmondsworth: Penguin.

—— (1984) *Deprivation and Delinquency*, London: Tavistock.

Woods, J. (1988) 'Layers of meaning in self-cutting', *Journal of Child Psychotherapy*, 14: 51–60.

Index